Mind Detox

Mind Detox

How to cleanse your mind and coach yourself to inner power

Deborah Marshall-Warren

Thorsons
An Imprint of HarperCollins*Publishers*

Thorsons
An Imprint of HarperCollins*Publishers*
77–85 Fulham Palace Road
Hammersmith, London W6 8JB

Published by Thorsons 1999

10 9 8 7 6 5 4 3 2

A catalogue record for this book is available
from the British Library

ISBN 0 7225 3647 X

Printed and bound in Great Britain by
Caledonian International Book Manufacturing Ltd, Glasgow

To Peter

Contents

Acknowledgements

I wish to thank Marshall, my father, for coaching and encouraging me; and Margaret Rose, my mother, whose gift of time and conscientious care enabled me to take the time to write on retreat. Thanks to Anthony Robbins and his seminar in Palm Springs, where I kept my 'Date with Destiny'. Thanks also to Belinda Budge, for envisioning the book, and for trusting her vision, and to Valerie Austin of the Austin Training Centres, with whom I finished my training in interactive hypnotherapy. And to Peter Lloyd and the friends who accompanied me whilst writing *Mind Detox*, and especially to those who read and gave of their time to comment on earlier drafts. Thanks also to my clients – whose wings have formed, continue to take shape and always to grow. Finally, my thanks to God, for sharing during those occasions when the voice of the supreme spoke through me, to scatter seeds in another form of words. May those words speak.

June 1998

The names and some of the circumstances of all clients herein have been altered in order to preserve their confidentiality.

1

What is Mind Detox?

When you need a physical 'detox', a holiday often comes to mind. You book, you organize, you travel to your destination. You come back feeling as though you need another break. What you really need is a 'Mind Detox', so welcome to the book and to the idea of Mind Detoxing.

The practice of detoxifying the body to cleanse it of toxins is becoming widespread. There are numerous ways in which people undertake a physical 'detox'. Fasting for one day a week has always been a fairly common detoxifying routine in Eastern cultures, and has now become popular in the West. Cleopatra famously bathed in milk in the belief that it would detoxify her body. A number of therapeutic practices that rest on the notion of gentle bodily detoxification are becoming widely accepted. These range from yoga to massage to disperse concentrations of toxins and thereby help the body to eliminate them, and colonic irrigation to assist the final stage of physical elimination. These, and many other procedures, are carried out with the aim of effectively cleansing and rinsing the inner workings of the body.

When you Mind Detox, you cleanse and rinse the inner mind. Your mind might have a tendency to run exhaustive rings around you with repetitive and fictional thought. Mind Detoxing enables you to coach it into a mind that has a ring of truth and peace. This technique is, in effect, a way of ridding the mind of toxins. The idea of a toxin is the perfect metaphor for negative thoughts that contaminate your mind, an allusion that Louise Hay first introduced in her book *The Power is Within You*:

> Imagine that your thoughts are like drops of water. One thought or one drop of water does not mean very much. As you repeat thoughts over and over, you first notice a stain on the carpet, then there is a little puddle, then a pond, and as these thoughts continue, they can become a lake and finally an ocean. What kind of ocean are you creating? One that is polluted and toxic, and unfit to swim in, or one that is crystal clear and blue and invites you to enjoy its refreshing waters?

We can extend this idea of a mental toxin to include habitually unhelpful responses to particular situations, or limiting images of ourselves, or self-damaging patterns of behaviour. It may be expanded to include mental scripts that block, restrict and limit our behaviour, that deny us a sense of freedom and true self-expression. It may include habits that we have held for a long time, but which we know do not honour the sense of ourselves as we really wish to be. Finally, it may also include unresolved tensions that speak to us through bodily pain, which can manifest through such forms as muscular tension, allergic reactions, and serious illness in the body's organs which for so long take the strain of our unresolved, unreconciled, unreleased emotions and then 'crack up' under the strain. It is a potent metaphor to think of undigested emotional junk food as damaging – toxins ticking away – toxins in waiting for their time to detonate the digestive mechanisms of the body.

What Mind Detox Can Do for You

Mind Detoxing has deep and general benefits that underpin particular symptoms, such as those described above. Quite simply, it can help you to find, and make use of, the talents and gifts that you already possess. And it can help you to love yourself. These are both notions that have always been present in society's spiritual traditions, sometimes as an underground river of symbolism, and sometimes bursting into the open. This happened, for instance, in 1997, when I had just started writing this book. A passage from the New Testament, Corinthians I.13, stepped fully into the public eye in a heartfelt reading by Tony Blair, the British Prime Minister, at the funeral of Diana, Princess of Wales. That chapter emphasizes the importance of love and ends by saying, 'And now abideth faith, hope, and love, these three: but the greatest of these is love.'

However important it is to love others, though, you should not neglect to love and care for yourself. The previous chapter, Corinthians I.12, speaks about our innate spiritual gifts, and in anticipation of the discourse on love, urges us to 'be ambitious for the higher gifts', and by way of introduction to the words to follow says 'and I am going to show you a way that is better than any of them': love.

Not only does Mind Detoxing allow you to cleanse and rinse your mind in ways that reveal your gifts and your love, it also allows you to sort and sift through your inner storehouse of memories and mental scripts. Taking the modern office as an analogy, you can view your mind as holding endless filing cabinets. You can learn how to revise files, to edit words, phrases and labels that are out of date. Indeed it may allow you to delete completely outmoded and inappropriate labels that you grew out of long ago. You may suspect that there is a lot of debris in there and it is going to take you a long time to sort and clear it all out. But you may be surprised to find that the first file you come across is so full of unwanted stuff that it is almost bursting at its seams, and disposing of it will actually shift so much, you find yourself smiling and feeling freer rather more quickly than you may have first imagined.

The more clear and cleansed you become, the more confident you will feel and the more you will shine. Imagine yourself as a diamond waiting to be discovered, perhaps covered in dust and grime, and surrounded by all those creaking filing cabinets. As you loosen and shed the dust and grime, and it falls away into oblivion, as the bulging files of redundant thoughts are jettisoned, you will find your thoughts are increasingly positive, clearer, more focused, and less judgmental. Your attachment to, and need to elaborate and energize, the negative aspects of your being will fall away. Your connection with your wise self will be stronger, enabling you to become more peaceful and more confident. As you experience an increasing sense of being secure, you will also become aware of a gradually strengthening feeling of wellbeing inside yourself, as well as a feeling of freedom from limiting fear and from the anticipation of fear.

You will feel an increased sense of connection with both your ordinary self and your wiser, more confident self. Mind Detox allows you to open the door, to switch on the taps and let go, and let flow out all that is ready to leave you – and to move on, to recognize and embrace 'the higher gifts' inside yourself.

Finding Your True Motivation

Motivation is a key player. For a few moments, be curious about the word 'motivated'. Motivation has increasingly been a driving force in steering our society towards the future. We are feeling beings, and we are motivated beings. Our culture tells us time and again that people who move towards goals and rewards are greatly valued in our society. Job advertisements seek self-motivated, ambitious, forward-thinking self-starters. This demand can encourage job applicants to pretend to be something that they are not – to say during the interview that they like doing a part of the job description, which they do not really like at all.

So often, our motivations overtake our feelings. So often, our innermost feelings are kicked into the net. Goal one – feelings nil. Goal-directed living that is won at cost to our self-realization can blind us to our true direction, our true destiny. Yet the new techniques of achievement have heralded personal goal-setting as the way to become what you want to be. The techniques of achievement are passionate, and they are persuasive, and they motivate positively towards material success. Such is the cultural distortion that suggests, sometimes over and above all else, that people who move towards goals and rewards are truly successful beings in our society.

All of us are motivated by something, and by some situations, and rarely is it just a question of money. Indeed Chief Executive Officers of companies pay specialists highly to gain insight into what motivates their employees. Motivation is championed as a thoroughly good thing, and so it is, except when a person is motivated without end, or motivated along the wrong path. Fear not – this book seeks not to decry motivation. Simply it requests you hear the calling of your inner messenger as she cries, 'I surrender!' to stress.

Seriously successful people can be motivated without end. Some are initially motivated to succeed by the memory of the poverty in which they grew up. Yes, people like these have made an appropriate and productive use of moving away from the past towards material security. But, when there is no recognition of their success by themselves, some endure unfulfilled motivation without end. Despite a wealth of evidence of their material success, they continue to spread themselves thinly, in setting ever more goal-directed outcomes, capturing ever more achievements as they rush headlong to become what they have been for a long time. They take power-showers each morning. If only they would take a Mind Detox to rinse down their relationship with themselves and the source of their seemingly never-ending stress.

We will move on to how you go about rinsing down your relationship with yourself in a moment. Let's take a light break to read a story that gently demonstrates our seemingly endless quest for material manifesta-tions whilst oblivious to the truth that confronts us – the truth of our success and successful living. The story records a conversation between a businessman and one of the indigenous islanders on the paradise island of Langkawi, Malaysia. It was a story told to my teacher, Valerie Austin, by an old man living on the mainland, and is included in her book *Self Hypnosis*.

A businessman was chatting to an islander who had just caught a fish.

'How many fish do you catch?' the businessman inquired.

'Just one,' replied the fisherman.

'How many do you normally catch?' asked the businessman.

'I only eat one a day, so I only catch one a day,' said the fisherman.

'If you caught two a day you could eat one and sell one,' the businessman suggested.

'Why?' the fisherman asked.

'Well,' the businessman continued, 'if you sell an extra fish a day you can save enough to buy a boat.'

'Why?' repeated the fisherman.

'When you buy your boat, you can save up to buy another boat.'

'Why?' questioned the fisherman.

'With the extra money you can buy a fleet of boats.'

'Why?' the fisherman asked patiently.

'Well,' said the businessman triumphantly, 'if you have a fleet of boats, soon you will have enough money to retire to a paradise island!'

Rinsing Down Your Relationship with Yourself

So how do you go about rinsing down your relationship with yourself? A crucial part of the process involves bringing you into the present – bringing you right up to date with your motivations. In effect, you will be reassessing your personal and 'emotional history'. This 'emotional history' is your own private narrative account of where you have been and where you are coming from, detailing the emotional significance of what you have achieved and what you have undergone. It is like your work history – your résumé or CV – but taking in your inner experiences rather than your outer experiences. Unfortunately, your emotional history may not be as factually accurate as your work history. And, as I have said, it is likely that your emotional history may not be right up to date.

Perhaps you know someone who has achieved many successes in life and is still being driven onwards to continuing success and yet does not *feel successful*. Because you do not feel successful, you continue to crave additions to your unfolding history in the form of more heavyweight job titles and work experiences. You may have stopped acknowledging your special dreams. You may have embarked on what you thought would be a stimulating road to success, have walked that road and still be walking it, having long wished to get off and follow your heart into something else. Something is missing. This is a story you must have heard before. Suddenly you are at the top of a ladder, but it is leaning against the wrong wall.

So why might you still not feel successful and confident in your success? The answer can lie in a word, a phrase, or a pattern of behaviour – often, though not always, learned from the past.

An experience of Mind Detoxing can be a small revelation, one that blows away all your uncomfortable beliefs about what you thought was impossible to reveal a mind-field brimming over with possibility and with comfortable and comforting beliefs in what is possible – if only you choose to listen, and cut through the crap!

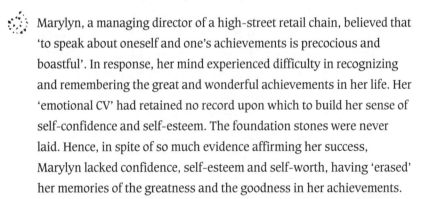 Marylyn, a managing director of a high-street retail chain, believed that 'to speak about oneself and one's achievements is precocious and boastful'. In response, her mind experienced difficulty in recognizing and remembering the great and wonderful achievements in her life. Her 'emotional CV' had retained no record upon which to build her sense of self-confidence and self-esteem. The foundation stones were never laid. Hence, in spite of so much evidence affirming her success, Marylyn lacked confidence, self-esteem and self-worth, having 'erased' her memories of the greatness and the goodness in her achievements.

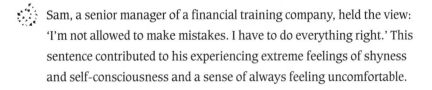 Sam, a senior manager of a financial training company, held the view: 'I'm not allowed to make mistakes. I have to do everything right.' This sentence contributed to his experiencing extreme feelings of shyness and self-consciousness and a sense of always feeling uncomfortable.

'It won't be good enough' and 'It won't be on time'. These sentences locked Anne in a constant undercurrent of worry and anxiety, even though all of the team in the graphic design company in which she worked had faith that 'it' would be perfect and perfectly on time.

Imagine: if you are moving into your successful future based on a thought or a phrase that may link you too strongly to a limiting past, it is rather like driving into the future looking through the rear-view mirror! In this case, you are never here *now*, you are never in the *here and now*. At the same time, what fuel are you pumping into the engine of this car that you are driving into the future? Would you run your car on fuel as dilute as you may now be running your mind? The habitual patterns of thought in your mind may be driving you forward on low-octane ideas. Nine out of ten incredibly successful people report feeling a lack of confidence at some time in their seriously successful lives. So what is in their tank?

 Fiona is a highly successful company director. She is well liked and respected. Her sentence ran along the lines of, 'I'll be found out … they'll find out that I don't know what I'm doing.' She worried incessantly that her company would discover she was not 'up to' and effective at her job. These words imprisoned her, blocking her sense of enjoyment, and passion, and acknowledgement of the truth. Accolades from colleagues were met with internal incredulity, and were lost in a dusty trail of habitual denial. The truth was that many in her midst celebrated her outstanding and deserved success. Fiona's legacy fuelled fear, and spiralling stress. Her inner critic and critical analyst seemed to pipe the sentence into her thoughts, so lengthening the period of her sentence. So it was, she herself deadened the lock that she could, of her own volition, turn – opening the door towards the truth.

We read, almost weekly, of famous and successful people, with life legacies of insecurity, fragility, and low self-esteem who are burdened further by words written in the press – words that feed their life sentences. Words that are neither nutritious nor solicitous in nature, merely scraps tossed under the door of a mental prison cell. Dry words. Daily baited bread laced with spite. When these words are believed and internalized and so feed the self's life-sentence, with little that can be done to counter them, the vulnerable self can feel besieged with self-doubt and self-loathing, further fuelling the sentences that rest on such phrases as 'no-one likes me', 'I'm unlovable'. No wonder, then, that many celebrities say they never read the words written about them in the papers. And when they do – tragedies can and do take place. The final sentence is cast by themselves, upon themselves, and they may even take their own lives. Celebrities throughout history have fallen prey to destructive self-sentencing.

Words and phrases oft-repeated, particularly before the age of 10, can become installed and ingrained like a reflex in your being, along with the associated thoughts. This tightly bound knot of word and thought will be triggered whenever a similar situation crops up, faithfully ensuring that the emotional responses run exactly as before. It will continue to rerun, until you yourself rediscover this silent and invisible habit of thought in the background, echoing from some long-forgotten time earlier in your life. How would it be, if you had a new way of gently persuading and coaxing some of those stale and outmoded ideas to the surface – and a way of accessing the team members of your inner mind who may need updating – in such a way that you could negotiate and persuade them to *change* their behaviour to something that is more up to date and true to the person that you are today?

Team Members

In the metaphor that we shall be developing during the course of this book, you are encouraged to experience your inner mind as a 'team' of many-skilled, multi-faceted emotions, qualities, talents and abilities, which you will learn to coach to create a coherent team for life. The team may be compared to a sports team, a family team, a work team, indeed whichever team feels closest to your idea of a team. Within this team metaphor, the good players are striving to help you enjoy life, while the bad, and the not-so-bad players, may be holding you back.

Are You Ready to Change Your Mind?

How would it be if you could catch a heartfelt feeling, sit down with yourself in the light and spend some time with the feeling? The intention would be to spend time with the feeling in order to discover why it is there, to explore what it thinks its purpose is in your life. Moreover, if this feeling and the thoughts it engenders are not contributing to a cohesive sense of team spirit inside your mind, then you can discover which of your inner team of players is not working for your positive and advantageous benefit. With that information in mind, you can learn to understand the team player, and coach it – you can be a personal trainer to change your mind.

From a deep-within state, you can ask: what is the reason for feeling that you lack a particular quality or, indeed, you can ask what needs to happen for you to recognize that you possess that seemingly missing quality. For example, you may ask: 'What is the reason for my feeling anxious in such-and-such a situation, or for feeling a lack of confidence?' Or you may ask: 'What needs to happen for me to *feel* more confident?' – which, amazingly, is the same as to be more confident. This question is likely to elicit a word from within. That word is the trigger for a short dialogue, a conversation – in the first place to discover which element of your inner mind is not working for the way you want to be, and then to discuss options for change, and to select elements or capacities in your mind that can be relied on to support and to nurture the positive state.

You may consider yourself someone who is flexible and open to change. Are you sure? Think about it for a moment with an open mind. Do you really change deeply or do you simply alter on the surface? Recently, you may have altered your hairstyle, your style of dress, your diet, your job title, your job, or your employer. All of these are examples of aspects of ourselves we may have altered. Altering things does not necessarily change us, unless our thoughts about ourselves begin to change – the thoughts that go on deep within our minds. Real, lasting change comes from *within* when we change our minds. Real change can be scary, *and* it can be the most liberating and freeing experience of our lives.

2

Designing Your Own Labels

As a feeling human being you possess many gifts and talents. These gifts are like the facets of a diamond – expressions of a whole. Yet, do you feel whole? How many of us are whole beings? More often there are gaps. We all have gaps. The majority of us seek to fill these gaps, with our work, with our social lives, with our material possessions. And, as much as we want to fill them in inside ourselves, the gaps seem to be getting bigger. We work longer hours, longer hours than were possibly worked during the Industrial Revolution. We have more things, and yet still the gaps get bigger. Is it any wonder that we often ask ourselves: what is missing in our lives? The answer so often is – our *true* selves and our *true* sense of connection with our divine selves, that which *truly* makes us special and unique, our 'free gifts'!

Marketing companies seek to focus our attention on anything but our true selves, our real essential qualities. The notion of a free gift has a very different meaning for them. We are bombarded with pictures of many 'things', which the 'creatives' in the advertising world seek to endow with qualities, feelings, personality, language, and an identity which may, given the right line of appeal, seem to fill the gaps, and give us a sense of identity, which we feel we lack. The advertising industry is a great observer of gaps. Advertisers identify the gaps that arise in our whole beings. Having identified the gap, they create a product tailored to that gap. They then give the product the same name as the gap. The product is fronted by a person who personifies the gap, acting out the imagined essential behaviours, and the spoken thoughts of the gap. And we buy it! We buy the whole 'act'. In exchange for paying a price that is worthy of the real quality itself, the product that pretends to offer the missing quality can be yours. Joy is yours! Peace is yours! Power is yours! *Happy* is yours! *Valentino* is yours, that seemingly elusive, exclusive, expensive feeling you can't quite put your finger on. Now you can relish the fruits of success by wearing the perfume around you. All this is filling the gaps. But for how long? Of course, when it runs out you can buy some more ... and more!

Advertising inspires desires. And yet more than one spiritual teaching cites desire as the cause of, and route to, great unhappiness. Indeed, advertising does not just identify the virtues. Advertising identifies the vices, and cloaks them with a sense of acceptability. You can buy perfumes with such perverse titles as *Envy*, *Poison*, and *Ego*. After all, they are vices in name only!

We delude ourselves when we buy into the advertising gap. We buy a label of someone else's design to create a statement about ourselves, either because the name or the label appeals. Or because we hope that the name or the label will fill our gap. At least, for now. So, we cloak and spray ourselves with a designer label, one designed by someone else. We wear the label that fills the gap for a time at least, and then we search for another, because it does not suit the new season or it no longer suits our seasoned selves. Our gaps are deep and wide and seem to take a lot of filling! When will we stop, and consider that we have within us the ability and the power to design our own 'labels' in our inner minds? The power to plug into and switch on a resource within ourselves, which will enable us to fill up with the joy of spirit and the spirit of joy, the spirit of being happy, and the happiness of spirit – to energize and equip ourselves with labels designed and fashioned *for us and by us*. Tailor made. Custom made. Couture.

When you are plugged into this resource you will begin to design labels in your inner mind that enable and ennoble your life, and begin to wear labels chosen with discernment and detachment rather than with the ravenous desire that is fed by persuasion from the outside world. In the outer world, one wonders whether truth, and the love of truth, is regarded as a virtue. In our inner world, love of truth and love for ourselves is the way to our discovering ourselves and our emergence into our full potential.

It hurts. It pains. It frustrates. It frightens. It diminishes our inner minds to think in terms of the labels we can choose to adopt: Failure, Shy, Thick, Hopeless, Greedy, Fat, Thin, Clumsy, Lazy, Big-headed, Precocious, Poor, Unworthy, Ugly, Boring. It hurts because these labels absent acceptance, love, and understanding of ourselves as created beings, never mind Liking! These labels keep us away from the possibility of learning the truth. In truth they conspire against us. Some of you will know the expression 'to blend into the wallpaper'. To some it will be recalled as an outmoded expression in the same way that labels that were yelled at playground playmates years ago in frustration and annoyance pale alongside those used by some today. Remember Twit, Nit and Silly Idiot? They were undesirable, but much less aggressive than those that replaced them.

Back to the wallpaper. The wallpaper in question was perceived as indistinct, lacking in both texture and variety. Monochrome. Indeed this wallpaper held magical powers! To stand against it rendered one invisible. Many of us have, at times, wished ourselves 'invisible'. At social gatherings we might position ourselves with our back to the wall. Blending. Bland anonymity diminished and restrained us, not having to face the unknown. A perfect blend. Invisible and miserable. Some of us have believed ourselves to be truly invisible when experiencing words spoken and actions taken in front of us – the perpetrator so seemingly oblivious to their impact. We can do our level best not to shine. Though we may diminish ourselves, however, we will not diminish the truth. The truth is that our 'interior' decoration is very different from that with which we seek to blend invisibly in the exterior world.

Just imagine one of your true special gifts, one of your spiritual gifts. Such as these: Love, Joy, Light, Peace, Wisdom, Knowledge, Confidence, Power, Trust, Patience, Kindness, Goodness, Faithfulness, Gentleness. Choose one that you personally can acknowledge in yourself and recognize. Now, close your eyes and just imagine your chosen virtue as a mysterious potion in a bottle. Imagine yourself packaging your potion in a way that is to your taste and represents you. Design a fitting label for it. Now attach the label onto the packaging. Could you now mass-produce and sell this essential you, the essence of you? Of course not!

Now open wide the arms of your vocabulary to embrace all of your virtues. Broaden your consciousness to create even more inner strength, more inner beauty, and more inner understanding and acceptance. We are beings of spiritual light. It is our natural inclination to be de-lighted.

Love, Joy, Peace, Wisdom, Knowledge, Confidence, Trust, Patience, Power, Kindness, Goodness, Faithfulness, Gentleness, Self-control, are our virtues for us to keep. They all contribute to our sense of balance, and our sense of ourselves as the best we can possibly be. Yes, we can design and create more labels, and we can manifest more fully those labels of which we desire more in our lives – both for ourselves and for the benefit of the people around us, our families, friends and communities. Love, Joy, Light, Peace: design these labels like banners, tall and broad, and made of a strong fabric, so that they always speak to us and through us in our thoughts and in our actions. They are priceless expressions of our special, unique, greater whole. These are just some of the qualities and virtues with which we can truly and truthfully fill the gaps.

Using Affirmations to Relabel Yourself

The chapters that follow will teach you how to begin to design your own labels, and then to design and clothe a whole inner team that will be wearing your true colours, and championing your true qualities. A starting point for relabelling yourself involves the use of 'affirmations'.

These are very positive statements that categorically assert who you really are. What happens in sessions with yourself is that you begin to come forward and create your own personal affirmations in your own words, your own selected vocabulary – having found within yourself the words that enable and ennoble your life. A simple way to attach new labels to yourself is through the use of such affirmations, for example:

One who was striving for an unrealistic degree of control

I accept my life as it is. I appreciate what I have and am happy with that. I am positive and dynamic, free of frustration and anger. Now I can feel the wellbeing, the being that is well. I feel relaxed. I feel good about myself. I am in control of the situation.

One who experienced a lack of confidence in her abilities

I'm saying I can. Everything is possible now. I'm gaining. I'm allowed to win. I'm gaining all the time.

One who felt 'stuck' in a situation

I am acknowledging and owning that clarity and precision. I trust my body. I trust my body wisdom.

One who was fighting her husband every inch of the way

I receive and give love. I care and am cared for. I trust and am trusted.

One who experienced feelings of nausea and panic attacks

When I feel ill I can cope. I reassure my mind. I am able to be strong with myself, to put myself in a situation and prove I can cope.

One who wished to experience fully the truth of her self-expression

I trust myself. I allow myself to stand strong, from a place of honour. I respect myself, my love, my intelligence.

One who wished to stop smoking

I take a fresh, clear pathway forward. I think about it. I give it time.
I say, I'm not going down that path again. I choose a road that is fresher
and brighter. It is easier and easier to go down the new road, instead of
turning back down the old. Smoking no longer interferes with my life.

One who experienced a constant battle with weight

My priorities have changed. Food is no longer a consuming thought.
I regulate my food. I am free.

One who described herself as being steeped in pessimism, washed-out and depressed

I need to be happy for myself and the children. I feel as though I have a
huge broom and I have swept out every cell. I feel so much lighter. I am
holding a branch of inner strength – like an olive branch.

One who wished to free herself of dizziness and shaking knees during public-speaking engagements

I'm cool, upright, strong and definite. My bottom half feels heavy.
My top half feels relaxed.

3

Inner Dialogues

We all talk to ourselves, though talking to oneself has an unduly bad reputation. The words are often rehearsed loudly and clearly inside our heads, albeit silently. Our inner dialogues are so alive and aloud that any radio or television playing in the background may be drowned out. The participating players in our dialogues are often natural mimics who have mastered tone of voice, register, and even dialect and accent. Their ability to step into character and stir our emotions is worthy of accolades and unreserved applause.

Stop and think for a moment, and ask yourself: what are you 'talking about'? What is the real content of your dialogues? What are your thoughts going on about as you wait for a bus or a train, or as you sit over a cappuccino or cup of tea, or a lunch-time snack? What are you saying to yourself? What are you reinforcing? Are you planning, or preparing, or anticipating, or worrying, or avoiding, or regretting, or 'awfulizing', or dreaming, or rehearsing for something, or remonstrating with yourself, or remonstrating with someone else? Are you asking 'Why me?' over and again? We carry out these dialogues all day, every day, but without keeping tabs on where they are taking us.

Some of this inner chattering may be about what is happening right now, but most of it focuses on things in the distance: what might happen in the future, or what could have happened in the past. Has the voice of wisdom ever reminded you that 90 per cent of what you worry about never happens? And have you ever embraced the truth of this wisdom, and the folly of your continuing conversations in contradiction of it? Perhaps some of your dialogues have become a merely habitual and unthinking response to particular situations, circumstances or environment? As if certain scripts of chattering are triggered automatically whenever those circumstances recur? These may persist as habitual responses even though your life has moved on, and those responses are just not relevant to the person that you now are.

Wings of Desire

Ten years ago, I saw a film entitled *Wings of Desire*, directed by Wim Wenders. The chief protagonists in the film were angels, mysterious beings about whom much is written nowadays. Although they appeared in human form these beings were invisible to adult eyes, being perceived only by young children and elderly people who may be close to death. Why is mention of them relevant here? Readers who have seen the film may remember that, on occasion, the angels would step onto the underground and subway trains, or wander through the silent reading rooms of libraries. There, they would listen. They listened to the dialogue running on and on in each person's head. Generally these private dialogues did not carry a positive energy. They were, rather, weighed down with fear, regret and anxiety. Gently the invisible angels would edge the trains of thought away from negativity and towards a brighter destination. The angelic minds would drop more optimistic phrases and notions into each person's stream of consciousness, like effervescing tablets plopped into water, and each person would find herself thinking in a more positive light. As they did so, the face of the passenger would be softened, uplifted and encouraged. As the angels moved along a train carriage, they would leave a row of brightened faces in their wake. I was so enchanted by this scene that I longed to see the film again with an urgency I could not explain. When I saw it again, I revelled in the simplicity and delight of the idea that people's minds can be turned around by addressing the language in which they secretly talk to themselves.

These were the thoughts of one male passenger depicted in the film, whose head was 'buried' in inner talk, travelling on a underground train in Berlin:

> You're lost, maybe for a long time,
> Disowned by your parents,
> Betrayed by your wife.
> Your friend lives in another town,
> Your children only recall your stutter.
> You could hit yourself when you
> see yourself in the mirror ...

The human angel tuned in to the despair, and drawing close, offered comfort and succour. Miraculously, the passenger's inner talk lifted, as a new dawn of possibility entered into his flow of thoughts. This about-turn embraced a belief in survival and a belief in himself to do whatever it took to survive and come through:

> What's going on?
> I'm still here.
> All I need to do is want it!
> Only then will I get myself out of it.
> I can let myself go
> And drag myself out
> It would be too silly if I couldn't do it!

When I first watched the film, I wondered and wished for this incredible phenomenon to be true. I was most certainly curious about the stirrings in my heart, and affected profoundly by the kindness, compassion, empathy and love shown by the beings, and the increase in confidence, and sense of renewed strength felt by the individuals in response to the small and gentle interventions.

So I touch upon *Wings of Desire* now (whether or not you believe in the coaching bestowed by divine intervention) because of the comparison one may draw, and which I intuited then without fully understanding it. We as individuals can listen to our inner dialogues and coach them with kindness, compassion, empathy and love. We can learn to coach them in ways that can soften our hard edges, uplift us, and increase our confidence and sense of strength in ourselves. These subtle changes can, indeed, increase our love for, and understanding of, ourselves.

Perhaps the time that you spend in downward-spiralling dialogues with yourself could instead be redirected, through gentle coaching, into a dialogue with a positive and empowering end in mind. Imagine some of the dialogues you hold with yourself. As a flight of fancy, just imagine that you could record all of your dialogues, onto a tape. Then play them back. Some of these dialogues are outrageous! Press rewind and play them again ... and again ... and again. Listen carefully and absorb the significance of what you are repeatedly telling yourself. It is as if you are brain-washing yourself all day long, programming yourself to think in a certain way – without even knowing what that programming is leading to. This is where Mind Detox can help you. The first thing to know about Mind Detox is that it is designed to teach you how to foster a better conversation with yourself, to engage in a more open dialogue with yourself – and to enable you to move beyond your current state of mind.

Dialogues with ourselves often go round in circles. They often repeat themselves time and again. More often than not they do not come up with anything new, they just reiterate what we want to hear in order to justify something to ourselves – perhaps something we want to buy, or something we want to do, or a habit we want to persist in. They are unresolved and unrequited conversations. There is a range of common forms that the inner dialogues take. We indulge in dialogues that are centred on the phrase 'if only'; or in dialogues that anticipate something that may or may not happen; or that replay old quarrels or mistakes; or that argue for an opinion; and there are dialogues that express inner spite, or pass judgements, or put up defences of our behaviour.

Your inner judge may engage you in dialogue at any time of the day or night, making its judgements and bringing forward the inner voices that express worry, fear, anxiety, guilt or regret. Those voices may lead to insomnia, as they do not need to sleep. They are players who play on our mind, and they can imprison us with their chains of words. They can prevent you from getting on with your life in a way that honours who you truly are.

When the child was a child …
… he had no opinion about anything,
he had no habits …

Wim Wenders/Peter Handke
Wings of Desire

4

Stillness Within

Relaxation is a state of stillness. This does not mean just sitting or lying still. It is about stilling the mind. A state of stillness is one in which the mind is virtually silent. Normally you may find in your mind a continuous hum of sound – conversations you have had, or may be about to have, of the sort that we discussed earlier. What we mean by stilling the mind is switching off that mental noise.

Mental relaxation is a deeper form of stillness than bodily relaxation. You can get physical relaxation by dealing with the outward manifestations of tension, as in a massage that soothes and loosens your muscles. As soon as you have left the massage session, however, you will find that you start tensing the very same muscles again if your mind is not also relaxed. In order to achieve a more lasting effect you have to still your mind. The experience which follows is a comfortable first step in helping you move into stillness. It offers you guidance as to how to participate in this simple procedure.

How Can You Still Your Mind?

Sit down in a favourite chair. Position yourself so that your back is in an upright position. Begin by becoming aware of your body. This might seem unnecessary – for, surely, we are all aware of our bodies? In fact, most of the time we are largely oblivious of our posture, and especially of tensed muscles. Just by becoming fully aware of each part of your body, you have taken a big step towards relaxation, for as soon as you notice clenched or tightened muscles, you can begin to release them.

Become aware of your feet resting on the floor ... the backs of your legs against the chair ... be aware of your bottom resting on the chair ... your back against the chair ... be aware of the air against your face ... In this state of awareness you are connected with, and in, the present moment. Now close your eyes for a minute, and just notice how aware you have become of your whole body.

The relaxation process described above is not meant to relax just the body. It is the first step towards relaxing the mind. How can we do this? Although you can focus your attention on any part of your body – such as your foot – and you can relax your foot, how can you do this with a part of your mind? The answer lies in the use of imagery. This is not necessarily visual imagery. Although visualization is the most potent form that inner imagery can take, it is a fact that some people are just not visual. It is perfectly possible to use 'imagery' taken from any faculty of the senses: touch, sound, body movement, or even just sensing the presence of people or things without being able pin the image down.

The language that the mind uses actually comprises sensory images and emotive words. To persuade the mind to relax it is best to feed it symbols of stillness. Begin this by constructing vivid images of a place where you can be still. A quiet, walled garden, or some other secluded and secure place is a good example of an image that is effective. The best place to imagine will depend on you as an individual. It might be based on memories you have of quiet, relaxing times you have enjoyed in the past, or it might be pure fantasy, or even something more abstract. You might choose to imagine yourself on a beach … or on the bank of a river … or in a meadow surrounded by buttercups, with the soft and warm sunlight playing through the leaves of a tree! My own personal image is that of my whole body suffused with light.

Keep hold of your sense of stillness when you come out of a relaxation session. Use a gesture, or a word you can recollect in your mind that will take you back to that feeling of stillness. Whatever it is, repeat that token to yourself three times, to ensure that it will remain securely lodged in your memory when you emerge from your period of stillness.

During normal day-to-day activities you may be less in touch with what is drifting through your mind. You cannot, however, deal with tensions until you become aware of them. A key element in acquiring and maintaining a state of relaxation is maintaining self-awareness. Try this. When you are in a room on your own, try imagining that there is someone else in the room just sitting there. You may find that this automatically makes you more self-aware. You will find it helpful to capture that feeling, and then to be able to connect with it at will.

Getting Started

White light is the beginning of the Mind Detox process. To begin, you might like to create a tape with the script for light visualization on it, and then play it back to yourself as often as you wish (see *'The White Light Detox Script', page 28*). The script is also available in spoken form on a companion tape to this book.

Why should you imagine light? Because white light is pure, whole and universal. It is composed of the full spectrum of colours. God said 'Let there be light.' God is light. Why not plug into this light force? It is there for you. The supplies of light are inexhaustible. You have unrestricted access. Inner light is not metered. Inner light is free of tax, free of pollutants. Why miss out on accessing your inner light? Switch on. Let yourself bathe in this light, become clean in this light, feel yourself re-energized and expanded in this light. And as you expand more and more with practice of the light exercise, you will become increasingly aware of a sense of an inner light that is on constantly. The more frequently you close your eyes and practise, the more readily the inner light will ignite and remain on, glowing reassuringly, like a pilot light.

The more experiences you have of bathing in this incandescent, cleansing white light, the easier it will become to switch yourself into a state of stillness and inner calm. And you will begin to find that not only can you feel bathed in light but you can also begin to bathe within it. You can begin to be still and stilled by the very presence of the light and you can – in a single heartbeat – sense yourself connected to a stream of light that provides a cord of connection to the earth beneath your feet and also the sky above you. This connection will enable you to be, and to realize the present.

Healing Light

The body and mind are one, and white-light imagery can refresh and even heal the body in a gentle way. It offers a simple, effective and popular form of healing imagery. You can send the healing light to any part of the body, be it internal or external, by visualizing that part of the body surrounded by light. You do not need to imagine the light doing anything special, or being different from ordinary light. If you can think of the light specifically as beneficial, then that may be helpful, but it is not necessary. Brightness and vigour are the important qualities that the light should possess, and the image should be made as clear and vivid as possible. You may find the light wanting to move: do not force it to do so, but just let it move as it wants to. People sometimes see the light rotating in swirls.

You may find that it takes energy to generate the light imagery, and therefore it may be harder to do when you are tired. If so, just try to give the light as much energy as you can, and let it know that it is welcome to stay and grow.

As the light becomes incandescent, and glows with its own spark, you should imagine the tissues that it surrounds healing, regenerating and growing strong and wholesome. As this proceeds, you may find emotions or memories coming into your awareness, as if they were locked up in the damaged or diseased area, and are now released. Feel any emotions that come up, and let them go. Do not shy away from them, but do not hold on to them either. Let them pass over you like dark clouds.

The inner mind takes this image of light as a signal to direct its healing resources into the areas that need healing. Although there is uncertainty about how this is achieved, it is known that the inner mind's internal language comprises symbolic images, and it seems that the idea of light is associated with the action of self-healing at a deep level.

When you have become accustomed to beaming light images at specific bodily areas, you can also immerse your whole body in light, either as a swelling glow of white light enveloping your body, or a shower of light covering you from head to toe. As the light grows in vigour, notice that it does not just lie on the surface of the body but permeates your whole frame.

The White Light Detox

Having already experienced a sense of moving into stillness, again position yourself comfortably on a chair. Spend a few moments tuning in to the ebb and flow of your breath. Feel the weight of your body on the chair, and relax yourself in the manner described earlier. Let the following imagery flow into your mind. Some of you will experience the white light almost like a video playing before your inner eye. Others will have a sense of light, a spark which you have to keep lighting. Do endeavour to keep lighting that inner spark. In time it will stay alight and keep you switched on.

The White Light Detox Script

Begin by sensing light, dazzling light streaming slowly down through the top of your head. Let this light comprise radiant, incandescent particles raining down as a power shower ... a light that is vivid, pure and energizing. Let this light penetrate through the top of the head, down into your throat, across your shoulders and down into your arms. Let it spill down into each of your fingers, then into the joints and your fingertips. Let the light pour down into your torso and your buttocks. Then let the light surround your lower abdomen and your thighs. Let the light swirl down into your knees and into your ankles and feet. Feel yourself a blaze of white light. Let yourself be switched on! Feel yourself plugged into a source of light that is energizing but that, at the same time, stills and relaxes both your mind and your body. Sense the light running rings around your fingers and toes. Let the light continue to cascade down through you – washing, cleansing and rinsing both the inner and outer mind. Imagine the toxins releasing, letting out negative thoughts and feelings that you may have about yourself and others, and feel the light working inside you. It may help to visualize a power shower at first, or a mountain stream, or a torrential waterfall streaming down. Just dive into a pool of light. Sense that there is an inexhaustible supply of light like a reservoir that is there for you to tap into, and to arrive at an increasingly deep sense of stillness and inner peace. This light, and your awakening to the light – as if awakening to the break of day – will bring you increasingly close to a sense of being that will generate a spiritual light of such purity that it will buffer you from thoughts that are not true to the beliefs you now choose to adopt.

The Lightness of Being

Julian, by his own admission, held down a 'reasonable' job with a high degree of influence and responsibility, overseeing a team approaching 100 people. Part of his role involved him in conducting job appraisals. 'You have to praise the best,' he said, 'when assessing the competencies and skills of a person in a job.' His beliefs were borne out in his encouraging assessments of those on his team – marks bordering 70–80 per cent plus. He went on to share that when he appraised himself, the ceiling for each of the same competencies and skills was 60 per cent. Unable to praise himself, Julian suffered from low self-esteem. 'I know I can go further,' he said. 'I feel I hold myself back. I feel unfulfilled.'

Have you ever remarked inwardly – or even outwardly – on a behaviour shown by someone else, and wished you had that same quality? Has anyone ever reported to you that you do have that quality, or a characteristic, a way of being that is exactly as you wish to be? How did you respond? Did you accept the compliment or did you reject it? Did the words inspire curiosity? Did you feel nourished by the comment? Did you feel acknowledged and validated? Did you simply feel that the person who made the comment was just being nice? pleasant? polite? But, in your heart of hearts, did you long for it to be true?

Could you just bear to believe that the wonderful comment was true? Could you suspend disbelief for a few moments to embrace the fact that all of the most wonderful virtues, qualities, talents and abilities you could ever imagine are already resident within you? If it helps you to suspend your disbelief, acknowledge that these virtues, qualities, talents and abilities reside within you to *varying degrees* – in the same way that a recipe may require anything from a 'pinch' to a 'pound' of an ingredient.

Some people are more cheerful than others, and yet we all have at least a little cheerfulness within us. Nobody is totally gloomy all the time (not even Eeyore in the Winnie-the-Pooh stories). Some are more creative than others but, again, we all have some ability to be creative in some areas of our lives. Some folk are more trusting than others and yet we all have the ability to trust: it is impossible to function in life while completely distrusting everybody. Some are more patient or more peaceful than others. But surely both qualities are latent within us, and can become manifest should we choose to polish and prolong their effect on our lives and the way in which we live. Believe! There is a bounty of jewels within each of us. If someone you trust told you that a treasure chest was buried at the bottom of your garden, you would get a spade and go and dig for it! Now, when someone says there is a buried treasure within you, perhaps you wonder just how balanced they are to be writing a book. Believe!

Perhaps you may feel weighed down by this treasure, rather than buoyed up and vibrant? No wonder! Many of the precious stones in the treasure chest are tarnished. They have become encrusted with fear, anger, attachment, worry, rejection, loss, loneliness, and a lack of love for ourselves that verges on neglect. What they need is a thorough detox.

Think about the qualities of peace, joy, love, purity, strength, truth. Dadi Janki, a yogi and an administrative head of the Brahma Kumaris, describes these qualities as 'Godly Qualities'. In her book *Wings of Soul: Emerging Your Spiritual Identity*, she writes:

God has so many qualities:
peace, joy, love, purity, strength, truth . . .

I had always wanted to have such attributes in my life;
however, despite my devotion to God all those years,
these qualities were simply not present.

Instead there was a lot of fear, attachment and worry.

Yet, as soon as I said, 'God I belong to You',

it was as if those Godly qualities
started to emerge in me.

That which was latent, again began to emerge.

All the negative tendencies left me.

I simply no longer felt that they were mine.

For Dadi Janki, it was the light of God that afforded her that recognition. In recognizing herself, she reports:

Light is also the light of knowledge,
the light of understanding.

That light allowed me to remember, that is,
to recognize my own true self.

You, too, can work towards recognizing the lightness of your own true self by opening and lightening yourself, by letting go of the emotional weights that shadow the light of understanding. Increasingly, as you gain insight and understanding, you will gain clarity and a sense of a light having been switched on.

Your buried treasure lies within. The process of Mind Detoxing requires that you turn within. You turn within to begin to cleanse and rinse off negative thoughts, ideas and feelings. These negative things may come in many forms: stress, tensions, anxiety, doubt, depression, discomfort, insecurity, and fears of many kinds.

The Orange Liquid Detox, which we will go through later on in this book, is a first giant step towards facilitating the cleansing away of all that stuff. Just as you may disinfect a kitchen before giving it a seriously good clean, the Orange Liquid Therapy will provide your mind with the tools to give it a serious cleanse, before you begin the polishing of individual stones in your new-found treasure trove.

Straight-talking

What I like about the hypnotherapy that I use with clients, and the Mind Detox that I am sharing with you in this book, is that it cuts through the mystique and mumbo-jumbo, and gets down to the real business of talking with the inner mind on its own terms. This is not about doing things slowly and gradually, piece by piece, skirting around the issues in lengthy conversations. It is about walking straight up to the front door of the inner mind and knocking on it loudly and clearly, and then talking directly to whoever answers that door. This is not about theories, or schools of thought, but about doing something practical and helpful right now. It is for this reason that I refer to the 'inner mind', not the unconscious or the subconscious, or the id or other theory-laden jargon. The 'inner mind' is just a convenient term for the parts of the mind of which we do not normally have full awareness. I am not concerned here with concocting theories about the inner mind, but with helping you to work in co-operation with it for your positive and advantageous benefit.

What I want to share with you in this chapter is the power that mental imagery can have to affect your wellbeing. Precisely how it works is not known. That it does work is attested to by countless personal experiences and by increasing numbers of controlled investigations. Depending on where you are coming from, the use of positive imagery may seem perfectly natural, or it may seem utterly crazy. One reaction I have heard from sceptics is 'How on Earth can mere day-dreaming do you any good?' Well, the means by which it can help us we cannot say yet, but the fact that it does have beneficial effects is established quite securely.

The use of what is called 'passive' imagery has been growing in popularity in recent years. By 'passive', I mean that you construct an image in your mind and contemplate it, or run it through like a mental movie. For example, you might imagine white light suffusing through your body, supplanting pain and discomfort as the dawn's light makes the night's misty darkness flee. We used passive imagery earlier, when we were discussing how to become relaxed. It is very good as a stepping stone to more effective work. In contrast to this, I am going to be showing you how to use 'active' imagery: by this I mean that you interact with the image and it responds to you: you have a dialogue with it. This is really a breakthrough in techniques for reaching into the mind and correcting patterns that you no longer want. It has been developed by several leading practitioners in connection with hypnotherapy, where it has been immensely successful. Now, a form of the method is evolving that can be used for self-help. Although working with a therapist can allow you to make changes more quickly and more deeply, the self-help method can nonetheless bring great benefits. You can also employ it to complement therapy, bolstering and reinforcing your healing process.

Talking to Your Imagery

The key to this is to give a shape and a voice to different aspects of your inner mind that are normally invisible but nonetheless exert considerable influence on the way you feel and behave. Seize the sense of the conversational stirrings and name them. The naming of the voices will help your focus and clarity.

Andrew Weil is a highly trained medical doctor who turned away from exclusively following Western, allopathic medicine, and has engaged in extensive research into a range of different forms of complementary medicine. In his ground-breaking book *Spontaneous Healing*, he records his encounter with imagery that you can talk to, in the form of 'interactive hypnosis':

> Interactive guided imagery uses the forms of hypnotherapy to induce a state of light trance and openness to the unconscious mind; but, more than standard hypnotherapy, it empowers patients by encouraging them to develop their own strategies for managing illness. It assumes that the unconscious mind comprehends the nature of disease processes and how to resolve them, an assumption consistent with the healing system's diagnostic capability. The problem is to make that information accessible to waking consciousness and to encourage patients to act on it.

The Bad Back and the Stream – A Dialogue

Peter was a computer programmer who spent eight hours or more a day hunched at a computer screen, day in, day out. This is a far from ideal way to keep the spine strong and supple. It was, therefore, not too surprising when, one day, while he was moving a heavy piece of furniture, he pulled a muscle in his back. An osteopath was able to rectify the immediate cause of pain and release the muscles that had gone into spasm and that were twisting his body into an unhealthy position. But his back was left in a weakened and vulnerable state and, a week later, he undid the osteopath's good work by lifting some laundry bags. This time, after the osteopath had once again set his back straight, he embarked on several sessions of Mind Detoxing to bring forward inner team members to keep his back safe.

As a logical, analytical person, Peter initially found the idea of engaging in creative dialogue with his inner mind rather odd. He rationalized it by saying, 'I realized that I needed to listen to signals that my back was giving me, so that I could look after it. Since I was not yet "tuned in" to my back, it made sense for me to use these imaginary dialogues with "team members" as a communications channel through which my back and I can talk.' He even supplied an interesting computer analogy: 'Modern computer systems always have a GUI (pronounced "gooey"!), which stands for a Graphical User Interface. The GUI is what you see on the computer screen when you load up Windows on a PC, or switch on a Macintosh. It displays little pictures called "icons". What you see on the screen, though, bears only an indirect relation to the computations going on in the circuitry of the computer: they are metaphors for what the computer is really doing. Now, these dialogues with the team members of my inner mind seem to me to be like a GUI for the brain. I know that, inside my head, and indeed my whole body, there is a tremendous amount of work going on, scripts being played and replayed, which I am not aware of. The inner team gives me an interface to them, but comprising mental imagery, rather than graphics images on a screen.

Through them, I can reach the invisible processes that are going on in my inner mind.'

Peter put himself into a relaxed state using the method on page 24, focusing his mind on each part of his body in turn, becoming very aware of that body part, and then letting go of tension in that part. He then engaged in a dialogue with his back, writing down brief notes on a sheet of paper, which he later typed up on his word processor as a permanent record:

Peter: Inner mind, Peter reports that his spine is slouching downwards while he is sitting at his desk. What is the reason for this?

Spine: The bright heat of the Sun makes me wither and droop.

Peter: Is it appropriate to speak to the Sun?

Spine: Yes.

Peter: Sun, the Spine reports that you make him wither through your heat. What needs to happen for Spine to be free from this affliction?

Sun: The icy stream of clear mountain water needs to flow up here and cool me. I am overheated, and my over-abundance of fiery heat cannot help but cascade down. This is what forces the Spine to be bent downwards.

Peter: Is it appropriate to speak to the Stream?

Sun: Yes.

Peter: Stream, will you agree to rise up and wash over the Sun, to cool her?

Stream: Yes, but I will need extra substance. I need more water.

Peter: Stream, I want you to make three suggestions to enable you to cool the Sun.

Stream: I must be paid for my help and services.

Peter: What is the form of payment?

Stream: Pay me with long, cool glasses of water.

          Drink water.

          Refreshment!

Peter: So, your suggestion is to drink lots of water?

Stream: Lots!

Peter: Please embed that suggestion deep in the inner mind.

Stream: How deep?

Peter: At the core.

Stream: How can I find the core?

Peter: It is at your source. It is where you come from. Will you embed the suggestion there?

Stream: I will.

Peter: Embed it securely, so that it does not drift away. Make it hard and fast. Will you do that?

Stream: If I can.

Peter: I know that you can do it. Will you agree to do it?

Stream: Yes, I agree.

Peter: Do it now, and report when it's done.

Stream: Done!

Peter: Sun, the Stream has agreed to rise up and wash over you and cool you. Will you now agree not to become over-heated and wither the Spine with your overplus of heat?

Sun:	If I am cooled, then I will not need to shed my heat over him.
Peter:	So you agree not to overheat?
Sun:	Yes.
Peter:	Spine, the Sun has agreed not to pour her fiery heat over you. Is there any other reason why you should not now stand erect, strong and tall?
Spine:	No.
Peter:	Will you agree to sit up straight, all through the longest day?
Spine:	Yes.

This dialogue exhibits some departures from the Detox Formula you will be introduced to in Chapter 12. Sometimes, Peter could not remember the precise form of words to use, and varied them in an ad hoc manner. That is absolutely fine, but you will probably find it helpful to try to stick to the suggested form of words until you feel more confident about handling and manipulating the detox method.

Also notice that the inner mind sometimes adopts evasive tricks to meander off the main thread of the work. Here, the Stream member was asking irrelevant questions about how deeply to embed the suggestions. Peter did well to short-circuit that digression by telling the Stream that the suggestion may be embedded wherever the Stream's own source was located.

I asked Peter what he thought this highly symbolic dialogue was about. His view was that it had to do with the fact that the office environment where he worked tended to get unpleasantly hot and stuffy as the day wore on, which induced a feeling of tiredness that manifested itself especially in his slouching down in his chair (which, of course, places a lot of unnecessary strain on the back). With the simple remedy of getting up frequently and getting a glass of cool, refreshing water from the water machine, he could overcome that sense of physical tiredness.

It is, by the way, often reported that most of us are chronically dehydrated. We do habitually fail to drink anything like the amount of water we really need to keep the body fresh and full of lively energy. No doubt the body has its own awareness of this, but needs some channel like this symbolism to tell us about it! It is one of the dictates of holistic dietary advice that we should 'listen' to our bodies. The detox method provides a simple vehicle for our doing so.

This case demonstrates dramatically how potent imagery can be. Notice, however, the key part that words played in the drama, too. Words have a potency of their own, which we will now take a closer look at.

In the previous chapter, we shook hands with the members of the inner team, but we did not do any work with them. They are still there in the changing room, keen to get out and start scoring goals for you. In the next chapter, we shall start the business of getting to grips with these team members. In the rest of this chapter, we will look at how your mental imagery can affect you for good or ill. This is really background material, but I think you will find it helpful in putting the team metaphor into perspective.

Essential Kit

A notebook or paper, pencil or pen are essential kit to accompany this book. With them to hand, you will gain the added benefit of being able to collect and weigh up inner thoughts in the light of your increasing clarity and understanding. Jotting thoughts down will afford you the opportunity to register your participation, and to recognize more easily how, by reading, by digesting and by responding, your inner coaching has kicked off. An opportunity to use your essential kit is coming up next. This is a warm-up exercise:

Self-image

The single most important image in your mind is your image of yourself. Just stop for a moment – and bring into your mind your own image of yourself. Write down the salient features of your personality, your lifestyle, your values, your appearance. Now, I want you to imagine what an angel would think of you. Who is this angel? Well, this angel has been following you around for the past few days, observing your thoughts and deeds, even your most secret thoughts. She is making notes in her diary about you, for her own personal use, because she is concerned about you and wants to monitor your spiritual development. What image would this angel have of you? Imagine what she would record in her diary. Now write down your chief features as seen by the angel. You are going to throw this piece of paper away as soon as you have written on it, so that nobody else will ever read it. Therefore, you can be completely honest, and include all the great things about yourself that you are normally too shy or polite to mention.

Did you notice any difference? You probably did. It is a fact that when people form images of themselves, they are usually quite biased. They may be biased in favour of themselves or against themselves, usually leaning in different directions in respect of various aspects of themselves. Most of us err on the side of self-criticism: we think that we are really not much good at cooking or drawing, or that some activities are completely beyond us, such as public speaking. We are like icebergs: only a fraction of our talents and abilities do we really acknowledge, whilst most of our capacities remain invisibly submerged under the surface of self-criticism, self-disbelief and self-belittlement. You can change that image. You can talk yourself out of it.

The 'C' of Confidence Visualization

It is not unusual for seemingly successful, high-achieving people to be singularly lacking confidence and self-esteem. Why is this? Life is often lived in the fast lane, and achievements – though they be great and numerous – are seldom fully acknowledged and embraced, or integrated within the whole-being.

Let me take you through another visualization. This is designed to bring you into contact with the greatness of what you have already achieved in your life. This is still 'passive' imagery, rather than 'active' imagery, but it is nevertheless well worth doing.

Now, sit down and ask yourself what was the first achievement you were proud of. Then ask yourself the second achievement you were proud of. Gather those achievements into a celebratory sphere. What colour is it? – what texture? Let each segment of the sphere be an achievement. Let that sphere become a ball of light. Place the ball of light in your heart. Allow the ball to smile ... to become a crescent ... a generous smile that curls into a crescent ... so much so that the smile creates a big 'C'. Now wear that badge of confidence in your heart!

5

Words, Words, Words

Remember the movie, *Mary Poppins*, where the eponymous nanny sings: 'Super-califragilistic-expialidocious, even though the sound of it is something quite atrocious'? Mary Poppins rather enjoyed the sound of sensational, sensory-based vocabulary. Your inner mind and team members do, too. When you are designing your new inner look, do embrace the part of your vocabulary that motivates you and moves you onwards and upwards – words like wonderful, exciting, marvellous and ... absolutely fabulous! Embrace and accept the words and suggestions that come from within, and if they are somewhat dramatic then just celebrate the verbal jewels that you are discovering. Trust and accept and notice the subtle difference in yourself. The more you are conversant with the basic script, the more you will expand your repertoire and range of language.

Language – A Diet for the Mind

I was approaching my teenage years when my father introduced me to Roget's *Thesaurus*. I can recall my excitement at discovering there were so many other words to describe the word 'bright' (glistening, brilliant, shining, beaming, blazing, burnished, effulgent, intense ...) or 'light' (illumination, radiance, resplendence, luminosity, gleam, glow ...) and I promptly set about attempting to use them all in a high-school essay. The startling arrival of that book into my experiential vocabulary ensured that essays took me an exceedingly long time to write in view of the many choices this treasure offered to a seeker of words. It also in later years led readers of my writing in educational and professional spheres to describe my style as 'flowery'. I acknowledge this may well have been true. In all ways I will always be glad and grateful to my introduction to this book. It offers verbal variety for each of us, far beyond our often limited vocabularies. It offers us a resource from which we can choose words that may garland our lives. It is sometimes said of someone who luxuriates in language that he or she has 'swallowed a dictionary', but if it can fuel your drives, why not? We have many, many nourishing words in our lexicon of language. So before you begin to read another book on food nutrition, how about dipping into the one that will enrich your diet for the mind? You may even begin to study the lexicon of love.

By the way, this does not mean tying yourself down to dry-as-dust pedantry, but rather revelling playfully and creatively in the Aladdin's cave that holds the storehouse of centuries of linguistic inventiveness. Our language is planted thick with images and metaphors, both ancient and modern, which bear fruits that are brightly coloured and scrumptious: devour and enjoy!

Why did I begin with this story about the *Thesaurus*? Central to the detox method is language. The method respects the power of language to change an event from the ordinary to extraordinary, from the maligned to the benign. Language can hold the ability to transform, to illuminate, to resolve and to heal. Words touch. We remember the beautiful words that touched us – those we read, or those that were spoken to us. Even those words that touched and inspired us when spoken on the silver screen.

The language we use to describe an event in our lives, be it in the past or the present, so often holds the power to keep us in pain or in pleasure. It can also hold the key to release us in order to realize reconciliation. We may be apt to say 'It goes deep'. Ask yourself, 'How deep – one foot, two feet?', and you may smile. The classic and oft-quoted example is the response to the half-filled glass. Do you describe it as half-empty or half-full? The choice of language is yours. Language offers the key to more than just positive thinking. It offers the key to increased clarity and understanding – if, from within, we can discover a word that may express and offer a reason for our existing behaviour. As human beings, we seek to understand why something has happened, why someone said something with particular words, or particular intonation, which lashed us so deeply. To understand, that is all. Quite often, with understanding comes a clear sense of vision and a tremendous sense of healing, and of being healed. The new word, be it about ourselves or about the person who was part of our story, may be crucial to retrieving the key to unlocking ourselves and gaining release.

When you have used the same word for many years, it may be a little threadbare. Take Pain as an example. Have you had an emotional pain kicking around you for years? You might consider packing her up in a suitcase and blowing her up! A suitcase is a shape that people often present to gather all of their pain into. They then set about cramming all of those outgrown labels generally designed by someone else into the suitcase. Lazy, Failure, Stupid, Scatter-brained, Shy, Selfish, Clumsy, Nuisance – you name it! Squeeze in those phrases and oft-quoted sentences too, those said by somebody else:

- 'You're more trouble than you're worth.'
- 'You're always in the way.'
- 'What more can you expect of someone who . . . '
- 'You never think of anyone other than yourself!'
- 'I can see it coming, you'll end up just like . . . '
- 'If you carry on like that, you'll never . . . '
- 'You're always asking for things.'
- 'If only you were more like ... He/she is going to make something of his/her life ...'
- 'What's wrong with you?'

(Whoever came up with the adage 'Sticks and stones may break my bones, but words will never harm me' was over-optimistic. She may well have needed Sense and Sensibility on her linguistic team!)

Sometimes it can be a tight squeeze to cram all the unwanted thoughts, feelings, phrases, sentences and memories into the case, and one has to assign Assistance to sit on the suitcase while the fasteners are secured – then you can blow it up! Can it really be that simple? Well, it can go a long way to freeing you and moving you forward, towards an increasing sense of freedom and liberation from words that hold you back.

Do you have a 'life sentence'? – a sentence that defines your life. Is it not time you got let out for great behaviour? You do not have to answer that question now, although you may find that an answer may just pop out of your mind! Seriously, if we use the Mind Detox to release ourselves from our life sentences, then it is likely that we can avoid inflicting the same sentence on our children, and they in turn on their children's children.

Once the sentence is acknowledged, you can reform the words and ultimately yourself.

Stealthy Changes

You may be surprised to discover that you cease to do things that you previously did habitually – you just stop out of the blue. This may not have been the outcome you were expecting. Sometimes, beneficial changes happen stealthily, silently and invisibly. As you reach out to do something that was formerly a habit, a thought may just pop in, inter-rupting your usually unconscious behaviour. You may find yourself having less and less of an inclination to bite your nails, for example, or to eat chocolate for comfort.

The curious and unusual nature of the thought, and moreover that the thought is to your positive and advantageous benefit, may be sufficient for you to respect it and follow the command. This work can lead you to transform positively and advantageously in many more ways than you would have imagined.

Whatever you choose to work with, you are likely to experience an increase in confidence and wellbeing throughout your body and mind. And having begun to foster the right approach for yourself, you will continue to affirm the work and to continue the reprogramming.

6

The Orange Liquid Detox

The Orange Liquid Detox is a direct suggestion technique originating in America and adapted for the UK. The technique is one included in the Austin Training Centres for Hypnosis syllabus (*see Useful Addresses*). I will now share with you this powerful suggestion that induces deep relaxation and operates a cleaning-out routine – and is an excellent beginning to doing a detox. Partly this may be because the suggestion contains a pulse of positive energy, which people can enjoy and benefit from even if they cannot let go of their tension completely.

The Orange Liquid Detox is available on a companion tape to this book, together with the 'White Light' script (*see page 28*). Alternatively, you may choose to create your own tape, making any adjustments to the script that you require to suit personal preferences. If you wish, you may change the colour, and change the 'liquid' to 'light'. With this option in mind, ask a friend or family member whose voice you particularly find soothing to read the script onto tape for you. Of course you may employ your own voice, though often it is more relaxing to hear someone else's dulcet tones, like it was as a child to hear someone else read you a story. Allowing for the speed of your reader, and your personal preference, the Orange Liquid Detox script will take between 25 to 40 minutes to record. Let the Orange Liquid Detox really do its job by allowing for the pauses, and the silence, and appropriate periods for the liquid to loosen the toxins and debris and then be drained away. Do it this way, and you will find yourself comparing the experience with a massage – albeit a verbal one.

Whether you listen to the commercially available tape, or to one you make yourself, the following strictly applies. The Orange Liquid Detox tape must not be listened to:

behind the wheel of a car, or any other vehicle;

in the bath or shower after a heavy meal.

Make yourself comfortable beforehand, either sitting or lying down, with your eyes closed. Do ensure that your answering machine is on if you have one, or that the telephone is unplugged. Alternatively, use a room where the ringing of the telephone will not disturb you. Sudden interruptions will bring the body into full waking consciousness too quickly. This is an uncomfortable shock for a body and mind that was in a deeply relaxed state moments before. So please take full responsibility for your comfort and full enjoyment.

People often ask whether it is appropriate to listen to the tape before going to sleep. The answer is 'Yes', but it is unlikely that you will hear the full tape before dropping off to sleep, although you will nevertheless derive benefit from the tape. I suggest that you do also listen to it at times during the day when you are more likely to stay awake in an altered state and so hear the Orange Liquid suggestion in full. In this way you will derive full and lasting benefit.

Indeed, the Orange Liquid Detox is cherished by people who have experienced difficulties relaxing. One man, who suffered a sense of panic whenever he tried to relax, benefited greatly from the suggestion. Actually, I had to use a modified version of the script with him. At first he was unable to make direct use of the orange liquid because he imagined the liquid as sticky, like a squash drink, so I led him through a version that employed orange light instead of orange liquid, and he reported an enjoyable sense of energizing effervescence for the rest of the day and beyond.

This example goes to show that we should never be dogmatic in imposing any imagery on the inner mind. If the inner mind says, 'I don't altogether like using that image, I just don't feel completely comfortable with it. May I use this other image instead?', then the answer is a positive yes! Be flexible! Listen to what your inner mind is trying to tell you and hear what it says.

If you presently do not swim, and feel uncomfortable visualizing yourself brimming over the top with liquid of any hue or description, do not worry. Others with your disposition have benefited as successfully by visualizing a transparent copy of themselves, made of crystal, glass or plastic, filling up from the tips of their toes to the top of their head, alongside them, or in front of them.

The script also includes a suggestion to the effect: *Each time you think of the warm, orange liquid, more of the restrictions and limitations will be released.* I often suggest to my clients that they keep something orange around them at home or on their desk at work to trigger this thought – a bowl of tangerines, an orange pen, whatever comes to mind and is appropriate for you.

The Orange Liquid Detox Script

You are resting comfortably now ... you are calm and relaxed. In this state of calm and peace, you radiate more self-confidence ... more love ... more enjoyment of life, because now you can free yourself of all the things that are holding you back ... all the doubt ... all the discomfort ... all the fears. In your imagination, you can do or be whatever you wish to do or be. Through your imagination, you can free yourself of all the restrictions ... all the limitations ... all the unwanted thoughts that have accumulated over the years.

To do this, imagine now that your body is a large glass

container that I'm going to fill with a soothing, warm, orange liquid ... beginning at your toes and ending with your scalp ... using your imagination, concentrate your awareness on your toes ... now just imagine a warm, orange liquid moving in through your toes ... feel the warm, orange liquid moving slowly through your toes and emptying into your feet ... now feel your feet filling with a warm, orange liquid ... filling your feet completely now ... and moving up ... up into your calves ... now feel your calves filling with a warm, orange liquid ... a soothing, tingling warmth filling your calves completely now ... and moving up ... up into your knees ... now feel your knees filling with a warm, orange liquid ... feel it moving in and out of your knees ... moving through your knees and moving up ... up into your thighs ... now feel your thighs filling with a warm, orange liquid ... a soothing, tingling warmth ... filling your thighs completely now ... now feel that soothing, tingling warmth moving freely throughout your legs ... becoming warmer and warmer as we continue.

Concentrate your awareness on your hands ... now just imagine that same warm, orange liquid moving in through your finger tips ... feel the warm, orange liquid moving slowly through your fingers and emptying into your hands ... now feel your hands filling with a warm, orange liquid ... filling your hands completely now ... and moving up ... up into your forearms ... now feel your forearms filling with a warm, orange liquid ... a soothing, tingling warmth filling your forearms completely now ... and moving up ... up into your elbows ... now feel your elbows filling with a warm, orange liquid ... feel it moving in and out of your elbows ... moving through your elbows and moving up ... up into your arms ... now feel your upper arms filling with a warm, orange liquid ... a soothing, tingling warmth ... filling your arms completely now ... now feel that soothing, tingling warmth moving freely throughout your arms and legs ... becoming warmer and warmer as we continue.

Concentrate your awareness on your hips ... now feel a warm, orange liquid flowing in ... feel your hips filling with a warm, orange liquid ... a soothing, tingling warmth ... filling your hips ... and moving up ... up into your stomach ... now feel your stomach filling with a warm, orange liquid ... feel every muscle ... every fibre ... every nerve in your stomach, warm and relaxed now ... warm and relaxed ... feel your entire stomach filled with a warm, orange liquid ... and moving up ... up into your chest ... now feel your chest filling with a warm, orange liquid ... a soothing, tingling warmth ... filling your entire chest cavity ... and moving up ... up into your shoulders ... now feel your shoulders filling with a warm, orange liquid ... filling your shoulders completely now and moving up ... up into your neck ... feel your neck filling with a warm, orange liquid ... and moving up ... up the back of your head ... up into your jaws ... and your jaws become completely relaxed ... now feel the warm, orange liquid moving up ... up into your cheeks ... and your cheeks begin to sag just a little ... now feel the warm, orange liquid moving up into your eyes ... and your eyes relax even more ... now feel the warm, orange liquid moving up ... up into your forehead ... and your forehead becomes relaxed ... now feel the warm, orange liquid moving all the way up to your scalp ... filling your entire head with a warm, orange liquid ... a soothing, tingling warmth ... just imagine your entire body and mind are filled with a warm, orange liquid ... become aware of a soothing, tingling warmth moving freely throughout your body and mind.

Experience a few moments of silence from my voice. Use your imagination ... and just imagine you can feel the warm, orange liquid freeing your body and mind of all restrictions ... mental and physical ... all the negative thoughts ... all doubts ... the fears ... the discomfort ... feel all of your limitations being absorbed and dissolved into the warm, orange liquid ... until you next hear my voice.

(Pause 60 seconds ...)

Become aware of my voice now ... become aware of my voice ... and listen. You're resting comfortably now ... you are calm and relaxed. Your body and mind are filled with a warm, orange liquid ... a soothing, tingling warmth. Use your imagination now and feel the warm, orange liquid dissolving and absorbing all the negativity in your body and mind ... negativity comes in many forms ... stress, tensions, anxiety ... doubt, depression, discomfort, insecurity ... fears of all kinds. Using your imagination, you can actually feel the warm, orange liquid working now ... like a million little bubbles inside you scrubbing away ... cleansing your body and mind from the inside out ... cleaning it up ... clearing away all the restrictions, all the limitations ... all the negativity. Feel your body and mind being freed of all the negative feelings ... all the negative thoughts ... all the negative actions from the past ... and the present. Physical or emotional problems will appear as darkened areas throughout the body and mind. Make a mental note of the darkened areas you are now aware of. Now direct the warm, orange liquid to those areas ... feel it releasing the emotional stress ... all the suppressed feelings ... all the pent-up emotions ... now feel it dissolving and absorbing the physical discomforts ... now concentrate your awareness on those areas most easily influenced by stress and tension: your head area ... your neck and shoulders ... your back ... your stomach to name a few ... now feel a soothing, tingling warmth developing in those areas ... feel the stress and tension being released through the gentle action of the warm, orange liquid. Using your mind in a more creative way, you've already released much of the stress and tension responsible for many of your discomforts. As a result of this, with each new day, you are better able to cope with everyday pressure at home or at work. Every morning, as you wake up, all discomforts caused or aggravated by stress and tension will be noticeably easier or gone completely.

In a moment, you are going to drain all the liquid out. Imagine now, there are tiny valves on the ends of your fingers and toes ... the valves are open now ... and you're letting the warm, orange liquid drain away. As the warm, orange liquid drains from your body and mind, a pleasant feeling moves from your head to your toes ... your body and mind are being relieved of all the unwanted feelings ... all the restrictions ... all the limitations you've been carrying around for so long. Just imagine them flowing out of you with the liquid now. Just imagine you can see it ... and you can feel the warm liquid leaving you now. As the last drop of liquid drains, you get a feeling of lightness ... a feeling that you've released a lot of the negativity you've been harbouring within you for so long. By the end of this day – definitely by tomorrow – you will have noticed a difference ... positive little changes in your attitude. Your opinion of yourself will have improved. You are going to feel more confident ... you are going to be more confident ... and it's going to show. You are going to feel free and at ease with those you associate with at home or work. Day by day there will be a slow, steady release of all the unwanted feelings you've been experiencing ... the toxic thoughts you've accumulated over the years . . . thoughts, from others, that you've accepted about yourself and begun thinking were true ... even though they were not ... you have within you, the ability and power to solve every problem in your life. In the past, you may have felt some problems were beyond your abilities to solve ... this is no longer so. You now look upon all problems as opportunities to expand your awareness ... to develop your mind ... to discipline your thoughts ... to achieve better control of your actions. These abilities are within you. You are aware they exist and you will soon find yourself using them every day. Each time you think of the warm, orange liquid, more of the restrictions and limitations will be released. You will be able to work with it yourself ... you are going to get all the negative thoughts out of your life ... they no longer exist unless you let them exist. They are no longer valid.

Continue to relax now and listen. In a moment, I will count from 10 to 1. At the count of 1, let your eyes open ... and you will again be fully aware, fully alert, rested and refreshed ... filled with abundant energy. For the remainder of the day, you may experience a pleasant feeling of inner warmth as a result of your improved circulation ... 10, 9, 8 ... you are beginning to rise now ... becoming lighter ... feel yourself floating slowly upwards ... 7,6,5 ... becoming lighter ... you are returning to the awakened state now ... and 4, 3,2,1 ... eyes open.

It is quite possible that you will go into a mild state of relaxation during the course of this reading. That's great! It's so easy to enter into a state of relaxation!

7

The Yellow Brick Road Team

Do you remember the film *The Wizard of Oz*? – dedicated to the 'Young in Heart' (and therefore to all of us!)? Recall the scene in which Dorothy, the heroine, is setting out along the yellow brick road with her dog Toto to find her way home to Kansas, having landed with a crash in a faraway place. A place far, far away, and out of sight of her known material home. Far away from Aunt Emily and Uncle Ted, and the farm hands who are her closest friends. Having longed to be 'Somewhere, over the rainbow, way up high, [in] a land that [she] heard of once in a lullaby', suddenly, she is in that faraway land – when, in a freak tornado, she bumps her head and falls into a deep, deep dream in her inner mind.

Longing now to go home, to go back to Kansas, where she will not be at risk from the Wicked Witch of the West, she is told of a good wizard who lives in the land of Oz. Dorothy is directed to follow the yellow spiral of brick beneath her feet, a road that leads to the 'great and wonderful Wizard of Oz'. Once she has found this very mysterious person, she must request an audience with him, and report that she wishes to go home. She is promised that he will share his wisdom, his ideas and his suggestions, and grant her wish to go home.

Along the way she acquires a great team of companions, each of whom is experiencing a different sense of lack within themselves. At a fork in the road, Dorothy meets the Scarecrow, who believes he is a 'failure' because he has 'no brain'. The Scarecrow laments that he lacks intelligence, and longs to acquire it. Attuning to Dorothy's conviction in the reputed power of the 'wonderful wizard', the two continue along the road together. They come across a man made out of tin – one who does not believe he has feelings. The Tin Man longs to have a heart. Dorothy and the Scarecrow affirm their common belief in the wonderful Wizard of Oz, famous 'for the wonderful things he does'. The Tin Man is convinced and joins them along the path. Together, they continue until eventually they come upon the Lion, who believes that he is lacking in courage. He, too, is enchanted by what the trio share about the 'wonderful wizard' and his wisdom and his renown for far-reaching powers. So, with respective absences of intelligence, feeling and courage – though with a conviction and faith in the Wizard of Oz, Dorothy and her team of companions continue their journey.

The four players travel the road quite unaware of the buried treasure within themselves. On occasion, latent and longed-for qualities speak by example, but the Scarecrow, the Tin Man and the Lion each fail to recognize the voice from within themselves and the ring of truth in their own words. They each lack clearness of inner vision and self-understanding. Each is in denial and continues to lament the absence of a quality, not sensing or intuiting the existence of the seeds of their success deep inside themselves. Perhaps you know someone who sometimes does this?

Let's consider the evidence. Do you remember the scene where the four come to the field of vibrant red poppies, with the Emerald City within their sight at last? As they romp through the field of red, commanded by the Scarecrow, Dorothy is overcome with weariness, claiming she cannot run any more, and must rest. She falls into the bed of poppies in slumber. The Scarecrow beseeches her to carry on. The Tin Man bursts into tears of emotion, *unaware of his feelings*. Moments later he even screams at the presenting crisis. 'This is a spell, this is! It's the Wicked Witch!...' reports the Scarecrow, his brain sparking into life, *unaware of his brain-power*. The Scarecrow seizes upon what has happened, not recognizing or acknowledging his intelligent analysis of the situation.

Eventually, the four stand at the door of the Emerald City. The anticipation and excitement combined creates a heady cocktail and the Lion speaks of his success. 'In another hour I'll be King of the forest. Long live the King!' commands the Lion as he warms to the feelings of courage, the body-language of courage, the words of courage. So empowered is the Lion with the sense of courage that he easily and effortlessly parades a vision of himself before his companions. The seeds of his courage are couched in a majestic display of grandeur.

Granted, the scaredy-cat behaviour with which the Lion is most familiar runs away with him when he enters the inner sanctum of the Wizard of Oz and he is confronted by the verbal bullying of the voice echoing around the chamber.

More importantly, though, the seeds that were embedded within his inner mind when he recognized his destiny are now scattered. What they need now is nourishment and growth, and this is fuelled by the further request of the seemingly all-powerful wizard. He commands that they seek out and kill the Wicked Witch of the East, the evil sister of the deceased Wicked Witch of the West, and return with her broomstick as evidence of their success. Shortly after embarking on the journey to fulfil the wizard's command, however, Dorothy is captured by the Witch's army. Together with the Scarecrow and the Tin Man, the Lion sets forth to rescue Dorothy. Curiously, as the trio approach the Witch's castle, the Lion leads the way, *unconsciously* emerging as a natural leader. The Scarecrow announces his plan, and *consciously* confirms the Lion as leader. As the rescue unfolds, the Scarecrow's supreme brain-power is made manifest. He shows himself to be a creative and masterful tactician and strategist. The Witch is a challenging evil, and – with an army of subordinates beside her – she has might at her fingertips. The four are captured again, and are now perilously within her clutches. With a menacing and leering glint she lights a torch and sets the Scarecrow on fire. Dorothy acts instantly to dampen her friend with water. The residual liquid spills into the face of the Witch and she is literally liquidated, melting to the floor, leaving no trace. No trace except for her scorched cloak, hat and broomstick. The last remaining 'block' to the companions' liberation and freedom is eliminated. Completely and absolutely.

The four return to Oz, full of expectation, announcing their success, and laying their prize catch on the floor of the wizard's inner sanctum. The Scarecrow, the Tin Man and the Lion remain *unaware* of their awakening during the journey. Up until this point, they have not acknowledged their individual personal transformations. Unbeknown to them, their inner seeds have taken root and flourished, and grown into full recognition. Although they have each demonstrated the very qualities they seek, their old labels – 'no brain', 'no heart' and 'no courage' – are all that their conscious minds are seemingly able to recognize and own, because that is how they perceive themselves, and how they have done so for as long as they can remember. Do you know someone like this?

None of the three have acknowledged how their experiences have watered and nourished the roots. None of them recognizes what it has taken for them to experience their longed-for qualities. They claim their hearts' desire here, bearing the proof of their victory over the Witch – the broomstick.

The Wizard of Oz continues to block their requests with his belligerent blabber. 'Why have you come back?' he demands, perhaps quite exasperated by the trio's inability to grasp the glaringly obvious? The Scarecrow, the Tin Man and the Lion, *if only they had noticed*, had already enjoyed so many *opportunities* to realize their newly discovered talents. 'I hope my strength holds out,' said Lion as he led the way towards the Witch's castle. 'I hope your tail holds out,' retorted Scarecrow, clutching another bright idea. Will it take a wizard to convince you that you already have your heart's desire? All you have to do is access it in the stillness within.

The companions, frustrated and desperate, remind the wizard that he has had plenty of time already, and insist on action. It is Toto who, with a paw-stroke verging on wizardry, pulls back a curtain to reveal an elderly mortal at a microphone bellowing forth his bullying banter. The Wizard of Oz is revealed in person.

'*People assume that if God were to talk directly with you, God would not sound like the bloke next door*' – this is one of 365 meditations inspired by God in a book of similar conversations that I will come back to in a moment.

And so it is with the Wizard of Oz. He is discovered to be just an ordinary man with an extraordinary ability to engender belief to help people change their lives by changing their beliefs about themselves. The Scarecrow, the Tin Man and the Lion are presented with pieces of paper testifying to their desired inner qualities. At last, each accepts and believes in themselves because an outside source, revered and respected, decrees that it is so. Do you know someone like this?

Do you know someone who is always, and has always been, studying towards *becoming*, or working towards *becoming*, rather than being and *believing* they have *become*? Could it be that studying and working are perhaps just deepening the known and taking them to a higher level? Just imagine, with this notion in mind, how much more present, how much more reassured, how much more grateful and contented we could be in the now, rather than chasing a notion of what we may *become* in the future. How much more powerful to recognize and acknowledge what *you are being* and **experience** what you are being in the moment as *you create it*. How much more empowering to remember and to validate your success of your successful self in the now, rather than to wait for someone other than yourself to present you with a certificate in the future.

The Wizard senses the best in the Scarecrow, the Tin Man and the Lion. So often we see the best in others and not in ourselves. '*You must first learn to honour and cherish and love your Self*' – is another meditation from conversations with God recorded in Neale Donald Walsch's book, *Meditations from Conversations with God, Book 1*. And finally one other – '*God asks only that you include yourself among those you love.*'

And what of Dorothy? 'You've always had the power to go back to Kansas,' the Good Witch of the North informs her. Dorothy, brightened and enlightened, reports, '... if I ever go looking for my heart's desire again, I won't look any further than my own backyard, because if it isn't there, I never really lost it to begin with'. This dawning is one echoed in Paulo Coelho's fable, *The Alchemist*. In that story, the shepherd-boy Santiago travels a world of adventures on a yellow sand road through the trackless wastes of the desert – only to discover that what he really sought had been literally under his feet.

8

A Constellation of Star Players

Just imagine your inner mind as a level playing field. On this level playing field are standing or sitting a team of players who run and organize your life. Through them you exercise your reactions and responses to different sets of circumstances and situations, like the ones that have been discussed in the previous chapters.

Spend some time considering which players have made a great and passionate contribution to your life. Think about which team members appeared to slope off just when you needed them. Just suppose you were going to choose a team to coach you for the first time today. Study the list that I will give you presently, and consider which of them would be on your winning team.

Your chosen winners may be losers for some. Your losers, winners to others. The list that follows includes many universal winners. These players have come forward time and time again to champion clarity and understanding, freedom and liberation, in countless detox sessions over the years.

Your winning players are those you choose to have on your team in any given situation or circumstance. The names of the players that follow are suggestions only, and will give you further ideas of the names of primary movers and shakers. Each is available to join your team, when you need help with a challenging situation.

During the selection process, you may discover that players come forward with the same roles and intentions, but with very different names. You may wish to note alongside any players that come forward words that have a greater ring of truth for you – words or names, maybe pictures, that pop into mind, and seem more appropriate and suggestive of these qualities to you. Write them down, and substitute them now.

Perhaps a knowledge of the positions of players in a sporting game such as football, hockey, netball or cricket may inspire you to begin to create a visual field of play to record your ideal team in a given situation. Examples may be a team to help you in a social or job interview situation or with a health problem, a team to support your drive to lose weight, to help you pass your driving test, to motivate you to exercise, a team to generate more energy in you, to focus you, to believe in you, to choose you. Alternatively, you may jot down a map of a 'changing room' into which you place your list of players before bringing them out onto the field for positioning, and a temporary 'no-changing' room for those team members whom you are aware are reluctant to change and whom you also know that sooner or later you are going to need to sit down as team captain and coach-to-change!

Your thoughts will be further clarified in the chapter that follows. When you arrive at the list, meander through it with a view to revisiting it. Some team members will jump out at you for selection, and others you may skip over. You may recognize the intention of some team members, and know them by another name.

This list is a resource to kick-start the flow of your ideas. The inner teams you choose to generate the change you want in your life will ultimately be unique to you – as you've read before, custom made by you, for you.

Use Your Intuition

Before we meet the list, we need to remind ourselves of 'intuition'. You can communicate with yourself in a very direct and immediate way. This contrasts with communication with others, which – although easy and convenient in the modern era of technology – is often distanced and distancing. State-of-the-art mobile phones of every hue, shape, and size suggest the ease with which we can stay in touch with each other, and yet many of us are not in touch with ourselves, or are out of touch much of the time. Moreover, mobile phones keep communication at a distance. Communication with ourselves is potentially on our own inner doorstep. All you have to do is listen and give your attention.

Another highly supportive and ennobling side-effect of this work will be an increasing ability to hear, and respond, to your inner voice – some might even say your 'divine, God-like' voice or presence, otherwise known as your intuition. It is not unusual for a person's intuition to increase and expand as the mind quietens down. You effectively begin to switch channel from without to within – to the self, and to discover the ability to tune in to your very own higher wavelength.

The more you become in touch with your sense of intuition and trust the insight, the wisdom, the suggestions, the more you will move from a state of inner conflict to a state of inner peace. Decisions will be made with increasing ease. You will move closer towards living your life in the here and now. Increasingly, as you maintain a presence in the now, you will find that just that moment really matters. And, when attention is with the moment, words such as fear and worry will dissolve out of your emotional vocabulary.

You may remember when reading the previous chapter that I mentioned a book entitled *Meditations from Conversations with God*. To begin to listen to a higher intelligence, to listen to God's presence within you, is the start of opening up to the possibility for your *own* conversations with God.

Let the team members Intelligence, Knowledge, Action and Responsibility or Good Sense take care of the practicalities, and live by listening to Intuition. And when you hear Intuition – run with her! Go with your gut feeling, your hunch, the inner urge, whatever you choose to call it. Follow your heart! Where necessary, genuinely take the actions needed to meet the suggestions that flow from within. If you receive a suggestion to write a letter to someone, some organization, or other – write it! A suggestion to contact someone, or to find out about something – do it! Be assured that the more you act upon the 'still, small voice' to which M. Scott Peck often refers, the more that 'still, small voice' will endeavour to make itself heard. In *The Road Less Travelled and Beyond* he writes: ' – the voice is indeed "still" and "small" – so still and small it is hardly a voice at all. It seems to originate inside of us and for many may be indistinguishable from a thought. Only it is not their thought.' By taking action you naturally provide encouragement to the voice to speak more, knowing that it is more likely to be heard. Trust and Faith demonstrably deliver more gifts to your life. With both of them in mind, you will find an increased sense of freedom from Worry and Fear. Then comes an increasing sense of inner Peace and Calm. Believe!

A Tour of the Stars

Meanwhile the players have already clubbed together into the following teams:

- The Visionaries
- The Cleaners
- The Motivators
- The Energizers
- The Comforters
- The Stabilizers
- The Meditators
- The Angels

Let's take a tour of the assembled stars. I shall quote the typical sayings of these winning players, which have been declaimed to me over the years in my work with clients. These well-worn sayings – you might think of them as proverbs from the land of the inner mind – will help you to discern the character or energy of each player.

The Visionaries

Creativity

I trust that you are a creative being. I can uncork your bottle. I can help put up your sail. I can let the sun shine in! I can help you gain your wings, liberate you, and teach you to fly.

Higher Self

I speak from a place of higher, loftier thoughts. I can see across broad horizons, and my view encompasses a wide sweep of life. I can see things in their true perspective.

Intuition

I will encourage you to listen to your inner voice, and to go with your inner 'gut feeling' and 'hunches'. Have faith in my voice. Do not allow yourself to be bamboozled by external opinions and ideas when you have heard me speak.

Inner Child

I am a child who loves to remind you to play, to dance, to sing, to write, to hop, skip and jump, to read, to paint, to cook, to swim, to go fly a kite, hug a bear, watch *The Wizard of Oz*, to eat ice cream – for no particular reason, other than the simple fact that it is fun and joyous to do so. I will keep you looking, being and feeling young.

Bright Idea

I will challenge the old ideas you hold about yourself. I will generate vital and bright ideas about you. I can overwrite all of the out-moded ideas and instil fresh ones that bring you up-to-date with your true self and the person you aspire to be.

Wisdom

I can ask straight questions, and give straight answers. I request you let go and let flow. I will encourage you to aspire to positive, higher thoughts, and always to look on the bright side of life. To think about the good things, the positive things. To dwell on those more and to believe in them.

The Cleaners

The Broom, the Vacuum Cleaner and the Duster Detoxers

Use us to perform a seasonal clean throughout the body and mind. We will rid you of cobwebs, and the layers of dust and debris that clutter your inner mind.

The Orange Liquid

I offer a powerful detox, acting like a million little bubbles scrubbing away, clearing your inner mind from the inside out.

The De-stresser

I will remind you to slow down, to relax, to be calm, to breathe deeply, to get adequate amounts of sleep, to exercise, to read a book, to listen to music, to listen to the Orange Liquid Detox tape, to go for a walk, to swim. I will remind you to let go of Doing and just to Be a Human Being.

The Motivators

Motivation

I give you a taste of the feel-good factor that gets you started. I turn on your sense of inner joy and enjoyment. I love self-improvement and getting you motivated to engage in physical exercise. You name it, I'll motivate you to do it.

Belief

I believe in you. I sense the best in you. I acknowledge and remind you of all of your best and brightest qualities and virtues. I will validate your sense of yourself as a nice person, a good person, a kind and loving person. I'll believe in the highest aspiration you aspire to in yourself.

Inner Personal Coach

I'm an inner personal trainer, egging you on. I can jump-start you, and stay one step ahead of your game all of the time. I'll exercise your mind, your body and your spirit. I'll focus you and keep you connected with the present.

Discipline

I can help you focus on the advantages of being disciplined in all of your life's situations and environments. I may come forward with pleasurable strategies and solutions to promote an easier sense of discipline in your life. I will bring you back to basics. Though I will be firm with you, I will also help you recognize your success.

Willpower

I will fuel your will to power your life, and sustain you in the driving seat of your life. I will make you go the extra mile. I will pull you through.

Future

The future is now. Put negative situations behind you. Now your bright future beckons, entreating you and treating you to clear vistas.

The Stabilizers

Stability

I encourage you to give more time to sit down ... to stop ... to breathe ... to restore ... to Be. I am a breath of fresh air. Breathe me in deeply, deeply, and more deeply. Together we will realize a more measured and contemplative pace.

Astrological Sign

I'll recognize all of the relevant qualities and strengths of your star sign – those that can affect and influence your success.

Letting Go

I free myself of feeling sorry for myself, and let go by looking forward to new opportunities and new horizons.

Control

I will help you to adopt a more relaxed control that honours your sense of self-expression and happiness.

Honesty

I sense your honesty with both yourself and with others. I strengthen your ability to stand and face the truth. I encourage you to uphold your integrity, your wholeness. Truth keeps you light, cleansed and free.

The Energizers

Energy

Connect with the light within and you will connect with a limitless supply of energy that is available for you to plug into 24 hours a day. I'll free you from feelings of exhaustion and stress. All I ask is that you sit down and Be with me.

Software Design

I can write any program you wish and install it, at your instruction, within your inner mind.

Goals

I encourage you to 'score' goals within the inner mind, to aspire to creative and successful outcomes, which honour you and your path.

Courage

I am brave and courageous and can remind you of all of the times when you have been very brave. I am able to act, without worrying what other people think. I do not let Fear get the jump on me.

Kick-start

I can get you back on track and help you finish whatever you began.

Heroism

I accompany you along the path and champion your faith to follow it.

Positivity

I switch off negativity. I acknowledge your capabilities and your potential, knowing that you can achieve all you set out to do. I endeavour to promote positive and persuasive feelings. I remind you that every situation has its positive side.

Focus

I help you to think clearly and for more concentrated periods of time. I can steer you away from destructive anxieties and encourage decisions and decisiveness. I will also increase your awareness and your sensory acuity.

Body Wisdom

I keep your heart beating, your hair shiny, and the windows to your soul bright and polished.

Movement

I help you put your 'winter' behind you, and move you forward on your journey through 'spring'. I move you towards a place of fulfilment, a place with purpose. I fuel your momentum as the wind fuels the sails of a ship.

The Comforters

Comfort

I offer comfort and rewards in ways that are healthy, and enable and ennoble you to accomplish your heart's desire.

Confidence

I promote a confident sense of calm and centredness from within the core of your being. I communicate effectively with myself and others. I nurture self-respect and encourage you to let go of worry and self-comparison. Be Yourself.

Happiness

I focus on all of the reasons to be happy. I remind you of how supported and connected you are with the higher aspects of yourself.

Health

Well, well, well – I will support you in your intention to be well, feel well and look well!

Humour

I sustain a sense of humour and of playfulness, which bubbles through your life. I fill the room with laughter.

Kindness

I promote understanding of both yourself and others. I encourage you to be there for both yourself and others. I remind you to be kind to both yourself and others.

Optimism

I'm hugely positive and free of doubt. I let go of pushing. I'm so many power-packed players in one. I'm powerful-plus.

Strength

I foster a resilience and a sense of strength within your being that helps free you from fear. I will nurture your inner calm, inner strength and inner peace.

Yellow

I sustain an inner garden of brightness and happiness. I love flowers, smiling, laughter. I will help promote your inner healing.

The Meditators

Contentment

I promote a sense of contentment within yourself, which allows you to listen to yourself and to relish small and simple pleasures.

Gratitude

I encourage contentment and peace. I seek to perceive value and benefit and gratefulness in all the experiences that seed themselves in your life.

Heart

I am a reservoir of unconditional love. I am always here for you.

Love

I'll help you forgive yourself, with love and laughter.

Patience

I slow you down for a while. I allow for you to have patience with those activities and ways of being that are entirely necessary and to let go of those that are not necessary and which do not honour your path and the way you wish to be.

Peace

I step into stillness and peace in a heartbeat. With peace comes forgiveness. With peace comes love. With peace there is another chance.

Time

I allow for you to have more space to Be.

The Angels

Acceptance

I find ways to accept, recognizing the gain in my experience. I move forward, leaving past hurts behind with understanding and love. I forgive myself and other people.

Clarity

With a sense of clarity you can make a fresh start, and start moving forward with a sense of crystal-like assurance in your approach. With a sense of clarity you begin to sense positive change. You are clearer about the work that needs to be done and take action to get it done.

Purity

I drive out blemishes and contamination. I bring unclouded vision. I brook no distractions.

Spirituality

I have wings to rise above everything. I feel the invisible currents of the spirit world, and I transmit their guidance. I am not tied down to the heavy world of material things.

True Self

I remind you of your truest nature: one who is joyful, loving, accepting, blessed and grateful.

Trust

I encourage and promote trust, knowing that the highs and lows of life are opportunities in disguise. I trust in myself and I trust in other people and their intrinsically good nature.

Wholeness

I blossom within a framework of truth and clarity, and strive to achieve balance within the whole being. Each of us is a trinity within himself or herself. We are made up of body, mind and spirit. We are physical, emotional and spiritual beings. These three aspects of our being are so different and yet so integrated that one part of our human trinity cannot be affected without having some effect on the other two.

9

Enrolling Your New Inner Team

Hands up those of you who have realized that you already do have an inner team – one that you've been accommodating for some time. In fact, you may suspect that your current team is in urgent need of a thorough detox – or in need of some serious coaching – and you bought this book to work out a training schedule to do just that. Pause for a moment and reflect on how the players of your existing inner team got selected in the first place. Over the years, your team members may simply have been chosen by other people, by means of thoughts from those other people that you were misled into believing and thinking were true, even though they were not. You may have questioned team members' behaviour from time to time, or it may be that you did not even do that, and you may or may not have sought to let some of them go.

How often have you been let down by a player in your team? How often has a team player pulled out at the last minute? Has a team player ever undermined your success? Has an inner team player sometimes just not turned up? Just when you thought everything was about to go swimmingly and you were going to perform really well in, say, a job interview, or a public speech, or a romantic date, or when you are privately resisting a cigarette or a cream cake – just then, at that crucial moment, you are betrayed and brought down by a team member who fails completely to turn up and play. Have you ever felt you could choose a better team?

If the answer to any or all of these questions is 'Yes', then get ready to choose a better team.

In your chagrin, you may feel tempted to blow out the whole team – lock, stock and barrel. But let's not throw the polished and practised players out with the also-rans and no-shows. Consider for some moments which players currently do play full-out for you, or indeed could be coached to do so. For example, to some degree Confidence will more than likely be on your team already, but perhaps you would like to bring her performance up to another level, to request that Confidence come out and support you more fully and more reliably. To be out there playing for you, come rain or shine – to be backing you up when, in social and business situations, it is necessary to enter a room full of strangers. Even to feel easy and comfortable enough to walk into a bar, a restaurant, a cinema or an art gallery solo, and enjoy your own company. Your aim may be to train your Confidence player so that she will automatically be there for you, holding your hand and supporting you, stirring your senses with an inexhaustible supply coming from your whole team's spirit.

Next, consider which players sabotage your success and tarnish your team and your sense of yourself. Perhaps they go by names like Anger, Negativity, Impatience, Fear, Guilt, Rejection, Limitation, Shyness, Disempowering Beliefs, Pain, Worry, Stupidity, Criticism, to name a few. The player called Lack may be rooted in many other players, of Love for yourself, of Respect for yourself, of Confidence in yourself.

Spills and Thrills of the Inner Team Rollercoaster

Before you commence the detox on selected players to let them go, let us plant the seeds of a new and supportive team deep within your inner mind. We will begin with the most important player of all – the captain herself! Before you actually make that choice, let us look at the responsibilities of the captain.

Hands up if you were chosen to be captain of a games team at school! Or, hands up if you were not chosen! It so happens that Physical Education was not my favourite curricular activity at school, and this was not really because of the games themselves, so much as the social pressures associated with them. My response to games was challenged by the tactics of the teachers who managed the team spirit. I remember the first time the teacher announced, 'In a moment I'm going to ask you to pick your team,' and I felt a sudden inner pain, because of who was about to do the choosing. My best friend quite excelled at sport, and was often called upon to select a team. Ever since we met in primary school, we had chosen each other to share everything, and chosen each other first and fast. Now Julie was to choose a netball team. She loves me ... she loves me not. She loves me ... she loves me not. The two captains plucked the freshest, fastest petals from the assembled first-formers. And when the 'best' and the 'brightest' games players were lined up, the few left behind were quickly chosen to conclude the exercise. Then, at last, amongst the dregs of the straggling players waiting to be chosen, Julie chose me. The first time this happened was, of course, the most painful. I understood she was picking the best players and I realized she knew that I was a loser at sport. Does that sound like a 'life sentence'? I remember my pain. It hurt. Of course, I wanted her to pick me whether or not I was any good at sport.

Dr Susan Jeffers often says in her book *End the Struggle and Dance with Life*, that 'It's all happening perfectly', come what may. She suggests that all experiences, when the learning is impossible to understand through the pain, will be explained at some later point in one's life. Now I cannot help wondering whether the learning is coming now in this phase of my life – the understanding that the team within, the inner team is what matters.

We suffer little narcissistic injuries all time: the rest of the world may not choose you for the games team, or the partnership, or the department team, or the stage show – you can nevertheless choose your own inner team, and so move more and more towards being a passionate participator in life. Now you get to be captain and choose your own players. M. Scott Peck asserts in *The Road Less Travelled and Beyond*, 'As a result of these narcissistic injuries, we either become embittered or we grow.' The best way to grow is up.

Head-Hunt Your Captain

In a moment I'm going to ask you to pick a fresh team. And I'm going to ask you to pick the freshest and the brightest and the best petals. First you need a captain. You! You alone are your own best captain. You can indeed wear that label well. We each have the potential to captain our team. It is just that sometimes we count ourselves out as candidate captains. Just imagine that you can sense yourself wearing the cap that says: Captain. Take the opportunity now and choose the best and the brightest and the most adept players to be on your inner team.

Select Your Players

Which players would you choose at this time in your life right now? Which players would you select as the best and the brightest? Which players would enable you to run rings around situations and circumstances that challenge and limit you? What names would you give to each of them? More than likely they will present themselves as names of virtues and qualities and feelings – ways of being, behaving and believing that reflect how you would like to be. Perhaps your team would include the ace player Confidence or Self-esteem? Perhaps Self-Belief or how about Positivity? Alternatively, you may choose names of colours that suggest to you an emotional experience or the desired virtue. Remember Captain Scarlet and his team?

Be spontaneous! The words that come forward may not be quite what you expect. They may surprise and tease. They may entertain. They may be naughty but nice. Allow words just to pop up. Some of the words may be ones you love to hear and use. Suppose, for example, that a word such as 'delicious' comes forward. Write it down! However odd, however curious, however outrageous or extravagant it may be, nevertheless put the word down on your list.

There are no right or wrong answers. This is not a test. Just accept whatever team members elect to come to the party in your mind. Let the words come quickly and intuitively. Trust that the players who come forward are lining up for you because they are the right ones for the roles that need to be filled now.

Go ahead right now! Spend a few minutes listing the words that label the players you wish to recruit for your new inner team. Jot each name down on a sheet of paper to make a team of 11.

Remember, you will derive the most benefit from this book if you actively carry out these exercises. Without them, you may find the ideas in the book just wash over you.

Different people may find it easy or hard to come up with the names of their team players. You may find that the full complement of 11 players is hard to generate initially. If this is the case, line up your team as far as it goes, and ask yourself whether any obvious gaps or missing links in your team are noticeable. Are there are any players that it would be good to have around, whatever the occasion or circumstance? Here are some candidates who might apply to join your team: Confidence, Self-esteem, Belief, Faith, Trust, Focus, Clarity, Discipline, Motivation, Strength, Courage, Truth, Patience. You might consider them as a family of players whom you would wish to have on your side, come what may. Whatever your image may be of these characters, include them in your team if there is a role for them to play.

Picking Reserves

Here you can add an extra two team members and name them. Which two labels would you hold as specialist reserves? For instance, you might pick the reserve players Creative and Wise. As captain you can make your own selection for reserves, or you might want to choose the two that I have just suggested. It is worth mentioning that I have found these two to be excellent at generating ideas when another team member has become lost for words. This may happen from time to time. A team player may simply be lost for suggestions, and be happy to consult with either of those two, Creative or Wise, and sometimes both. You may trust that at least one of them will offer counsel when the time comes.

Creative and Wise are especially good at this. And, yes, we do all have these players available to us. I acknowledge that some readers will be speechless with astonishment, denying that Creative could ever be manifested on their inner team. Rest assured that she is a real presence, although she may need just a little exercise and encouragement to help her shine. Perhaps you relegated her to the junior league when a voice announced you were not very good at drawing or singing at 10 years of age. Most of us just need to reframe our perception of how we view creativity. Creativity enters into so many of our day-to-day decisions. You are creative when you 'creatively' perform tasks in your own special idiosyncratic way. That really is being creative!

You may imagine Wise as a sage of some sort, or as a large, dusty, leather-bound book from which you need to remember to brush the dust from time to time to gain access to the wisdom that it holds. Those pages may provide the wisdom to illuminate the dusty paths leading in directions that you have long forgotten, and on which layers of stress, tension or stifling self-criticism have settled over the years.

Get ready – for Creative and Wise are ready to move the team into a higher league. As you detox with increasing ease, you will find these two players step out onto your inner mind-field time and again. They will be two of the most supportive players in your team, reliable and to be relied upon.

Training with the Team

Having chosen your team, as captain, it is now time for you to embark on the first stages of coaching. I am going to share with you how to begin to learn from your inner team. I am going to share how to invite them forward and how to learn to seek their counsel.

You now need to relax yourself, for example in the manner that I described earlier (*see page 28*) or by following the routine below. Sit down where you can be alone, where nobody will disturb you. Ensure the answering machine is on, or that the telephone is temporarily disengaged. Close your eyes. Very slowly take three deep breaths. Slowly count backwards from ten to one. Imagine yourself in a very restful place, a favourite room, at the seaside, in the mountains, on a sailing boat, or in a garden. Wherever is your favourite place, go there now. You can make-believe the place if you like. Your body cannot tell the difference between real or imagined experiences if they are vivid enough. Let yourself enjoy the place you have chosen. When your thoughts wander, just refocus, and when your thoughts wander again, just refocus again, and again as necessary.

Bring to mind one member of your team. It could be any member. Trust that the member who comes forward first is absolutely fine. Sense the presence of the player in yourself. Feel it in the core of your being, not just in your head. Thank the team player for coming forward. Ask the team player for an idea or a suggestion that will help you in your current situation or circumstance. Wait for the reply. The reply may not be what you expect to hear. Just accept it anyway. Thank the team player for her suggestion.

Bring to mind a second member of your team. Again, it could be any member. Once more, trust that the member that comes forward is absolutely fine. Sense the presence of the player in yourself. Again, thank the team player for coming forward. As before, ask the team player for an idea or a suggestion that will help you in your current situation or circumstance. Wait for the reply. The reply may not be what you expect to hear. Just accept it. Thank the team player for her suggestion. Finally, repeat this process for a third team member, so that you will have three suggestions altogether.

Each suggestion may come forward as one word. The word may even be a repetition of the name of the presenting team member. It may come forward as a phrase comprising one or two words. It may be a sentence. Occasionally as a symbol of the quality or virtue. Much has been written about symbology, especially symbols encountered in dreams. Of particular importance when Mind-Detoxing is to ask yourself what the symbol means to you. As an illustration let's first hear from three team members each promoting Confidence:

Suggestions as short words or phrases:

- Be yourself.
- Don't compare.
- Let go.

Suggestions as sentences:

- Trusting that I have as much to offer other people as they have to me.
- Being more relaxed about believing that my own views are important.
- Feeling that people like me for who I am and they are not pushing for more.

Symbolic suggestions:

- Sword.
- Shield.
- Helmet.

And now from three encouraging a sense of Security:
Suggestions as short words or phrases:

- Courage.
- Protection.
- Self-belief.

Suggestions as sentences:

- I take on all of the stress.
- I don't have to be that way.
- I choose to be different.

Symbolic suggestions:

- Planting new seeds.
- Building a strong house.
- A view – light and sunshine.

And lastly, three instilling Relaxation.
Suggestions as short words or phrases:

- Sink down.
- Float away.
- Just be.

Suggestions as sentences:

- I send all my worries away on a long trip.
- I create a special time just for myself.
- I rest, and restore my strength.

Symbolic suggestions:

- Beach.
- Ocean.
- Foam-filled bathtub.

Invite as many chosen team members as you wish to come forward with their suggestion(s), thanking each for their ideas. Continue this process until you sense you have gained an increased degree of clarity and understanding from within. A sense of clarity and understanding made possible by a 'body' of opinion from within. A clarity and understanding that has invoked some nutritional thoughts and words to empower, ennoble and enable your life in the moment.

Bringing in the Reserves

When a team player offers no suggestions, no ideas, then you can invite your reserve players, who may be Creative or Wise, to come forward. Thank whichever reserve player comes forward. Ask the reserve to share her idea or suggestion with the silent player, and for the silent player to hear what needs to be heard. Listen for whatever comes forward. Thank both team members for their sharing.

Cutting out the Motormouth

In the early stages of the detox process, it is natural for a player called Talkative to interrupt from time to time. Talkative uses diversionary tactics to distract you from your coaching. She may pick up on a team player like Delicious, get a taste for deliciousness, and then set forth imagining, say, a cream tea with the team once she has finished talking with them. She can pick up on a player's word in mid-sentence and sweep you off on a reverie, a list-making exercise. In an instant she can end your briefing, and take you off on a verbal shopping spree. Initially, she takes you off window shopping, harmless enough, casting around for associated stories, memories and conversations. Then she is inside the shop, buried under the imaginings, the tales and the telling of them, and she has bought the imagined ending, and has experienced the outcome in her wanderings. All this, without the benefit of any input from her team. For, in the midst of this melange of inner dialogue, the other team members have sloped off, back to the no-changing room.

As you may discover, she can have a tendency to take over from the captain. So, you must stick with, and support, your team in the training. Do not let her run away with your team's train of thought. Keep on coaching, and your inner team will become more and more exercised and consequently fitter and fitter.

In subsequent initial inner team briefings you may invite one or more players from the family known as Inner Retreat. They go by names such as these: Stillness, Peace, Quiet, Contentment, and Silence. Call upon one or more of them to join your team. Whatever name the player presents to you, accept this player and its way of being onto your inner team, and take on board that player's quality. The quality or feeling may come forward as a shape, or as a natural form, for example a Tree, a Babbling Brook, a River, a Hummingbird, Sand or Sea – an added aspect of your quiet place. As you breathe in, breathe in a sense of the Tree, and as you breathe out, breathe out Talkative, letting go of the distracting whispers, conversations, lists and wandering wonderings that intrude. Come back to the quality of the Tree, the Brook, the River, the Hummingbird, the Sand or the Sea. And Be. Then call upon another team player and ask her to come forward and share a word, a phrase, an idea, a suggestion. In this way the peaceful players will enable you to maintain a sense of calm, a sense of peace – such that the voice of the player may be heard, and absorbed, embedded deep in your inner mind.

Reflecting on the Team

Having spoken with as many members of your chosen team as you have time and need for, notice the difference in yourself. Perhaps you feel an increased sense of lightness, of clarity, of direction, of calm, of perspective?

Bear in mind the deeper you go in counsel, the more relaxed you will be, and the more relaxed you sense yourself to be, the deeper and more profound will be the team briefing and the feedback that results from it.

How a State of Contemplation Feels

How is the contemplative state of mind likely to feel? In this altered state of contemplation you are not asleep and are aware of everything that is going on. It is a kind of prayerful state. You may give the impression of being asleep because your body is relaxed.

Let me give you a comparison. Daydreaming is a heightened state of awareness. You change gear in your mind to go into a daydream. If you stay in that daydream, and become completely involved in it, you will be quite oblivious to what is happening around you. Because your inner mind is acting for your survival, your inner mind steps forward as a watchful observer – in effect to protect you – if some external danger arises that requires your immediate full consciousness.

Another example is driving your car on the motorway. More than likely you can recollect an experience of becoming deeply involved in a thought or daydream to the extent that you ceased to notice the traffic passing or the scenery. It is possible to drive a good few miles like this and then suddenly come to full awareness and realize that you could have had an accident. Be reassured that had the car in front put its brake lights on, then the inner mind would have immediately brought the conscious mind back in a fraction of a second to deal with the threat to survival. You may call this state autopilot. When tragedies do occur, it is usually because the driver has fallen asleep at the wheel. On British motorways today you will increasingly see signs that announce 'Tiredness Kills'. When you are tired, follow the command and take a break.

In a state of deep stillness you are able to gain rapport with the inner mind to enable a suggestion to be installed free of criticism and doubt, in order to build a new program.

[In your contemplative state,] your inner mind – for your benefit – takes note of what is happening around you. The suggestions [that come forward from team members] are all for your benefit, and go directly into your inner mind. There they are accepted, because the ideas are for your benefit. Thoughts become firmly fixed deep in your inner mind – embedded, so they remain with you, long after you have opened your eyes – helping your inner being to change those things you want to change for your own sake.

Adapted from *Free Yourself from Fear*, by Valerie Austin.

About the Suggestions

No Suggestions?

Accessing the inner mind is a little bit like a word-association game. Do not worry or concern yourself that the suggestions may not make sense. Some suggestions will pop in as symbols, and you will wonder 'Where on earth did that come from?' Perhaps it didn't come from earth? Accept it anyway. When your inner mind does not come up with anything ... stay with it. The natural curiosity of the mind precludes it from staying blank for long. Blankness is your longer-term outcome. You will come to notice that, as you truly let go of the rogue team members, the internal dialogue in your inner mind will become less and less. Your thoughts will concern themselves with the truer aspects of your inner being. Increasingly, you will feel cleansed, and so cleaner and clearer and more focused in outlook.

'I Can't Remember the Suggestions'

It may seem unlikely that you would be unable to remember the suggestions offered by team members, given that there are generally only three suggestions to recall, but sometimes it does happen – the words that floated into your mind and sparkled there with their seeming sense and self-empowerment are gone! You simply cannot remember the pearls of wisdom. Sometimes, they disappear as thoroughly as dreams do. (Have you ever felt that sense of impotent frustration early in the morning, when you know that you have had a fascinating and vivid dream, but now it completely escapes your recollection? Well, occasionally, that message that comes to you from your inner mind vanishes in the same way.) Yes, it does feel like a frustration! As you become more conversant with the detox method and the entrusting of the inner mind and her capacity to offer guidance, you will find that words come in as though carried by a breeze – held before you for acknowledgement and agreement and then gone – as though transported far away by the same wind of change that brought them before you.

'How Do I Know the Suggestions Have Gone in?'

How can you be sure that the suggestions really have been embedded firmly in the inner mind, and that they will actually take effect? Again, the secret is trust: just trust that the words, and the pearls of wisdom that are strung onto them, are embedded deep within your inner mind and that the work will be done, and then notice the difference. The suggestions are anchored at a very deep level. It is not unusual sometimes for this work to resemble a kind of inner prayer or meditation. Count your blessings and consider the words that have been bestowed within you.

Alternatives to the Word 'Suggestions'

'Suggestions' is one option, and the one I have chosen to use for purposes of creating the basic script. You could, however, introduce the word 'commands' or 'commitments'. Another option may be 'wisdom'. You would then tell your inner mind to 'embed that wisdom deep within'. The basic script is there for you to develop, expand, and make your own.

More, or Fewer, Than Three Suggestions

When more than three suggestions come forward, then – provided that each accords with your positive and advantageous good – embrace all those offered and plant them all deep within your inner mind. The basic script is there for you to get started. Undoubtedly, as you expand and grow within, the detox method will grow with you.

If just a single suggestion comes forward, then proceed on the basis that this one suggestion offers profound nutrition, of such potency that on its own it can promote your success. Go forward with that single quality, free of concern about the quantity.

When you are familiar with the detox process, there are team members whom you may invoke to generate more suggestions if you choose. As you've already discovered, the two team players who have proven especially good at this are called Creative and Wise, whom we have discussed earlier.

In Conclusion

You have now created a whole, and wholly new, team who are committed to playing their level-best for you. In the next chapter, you will perform the necessary reverse task of disbanding the old inner team, who never gave their all for you and to whom you will feel a dissolving sense of attachment.

10

Disbanding Your Old Inner Team

Amongst the rank and file of our inner team are always going to lurk negative and unsupportive players that frustrate our pathway towards peaceful self-expression. I touched upon some of these rogue players in the previous chapter. Is it not curious that, as their captain, you still tolerate them at all? Given the opportunity to line them all up and frog-march them off the inner playing field, many of us would jump at the chance. Unfortunately, this would probably present a challenge because some of them may refuse to go. Protest you might, but some would stay put.

Many of these unsupportive players reside in your old team, some of whom are surely ready to be detoxed from your inner mind. The Orange Liquid Detox is a first step towards flushing them out. This process will loosen their hold over you and ease the process of elimination one by one. Just like the Wicked Witch of the West, they represent blocks to your success and must be liquidated.

Spend as long as you like examining the team members on your list and prioritize their elimination.

You may have inherited some of the old team members – learned, chosen through circumstances, situations and events way back when. Some may well be part of a *life* sentence. Here are the names of some of the usual suspects, a motley bunch of rogue players who have been thrown out by clients I have worked with in the past: Fear, Resentment,

Anxiety, Discouragement, Worry, Punishment, Insecurity, Struggle, Grievances, Nervousness, Self-consciousness, Limitation – and last, but not least, a sense of being Unimportant.

Work with one or two players each day. The intention is not to eliminate all the suspected rogue players in one single swoop! The process of elimination or transfer, as you will discover, is a project, and may take several sessions and concentrated effort. Allow repeat sessions for those long-standing team members who prove more resistant than others.

Choose the first on your list to begin with. The task is to take them in one by one; to examine them and, in the course of examining them, examine yourself. What follows is a process of lightening, a process that enables you, with repeated practice, to off-load the free-loaders. This detox strategy will enable you to liquidate those players who do not honour the person you are now.

It is a process that will help update your emotional CV or résumé. As you let go, you will move towards a sense of lightness, liberation and freedom. This is because, having released them, you let go of the rogues and also-rans, creating space for new and vital growth and talent. It is important to top up your team – to transfer in your brightest stars! This helps ensure the old rogues will not easily find room to regain their position. Your transfers are your best and most polished players, the jewels on your team. They gain promotion to a higher league and eventually gain their wings.

The process that follows offers an alternative to the white-light script. You may choose to dive into the white-light contemplation, as provided in Chapter 4, and consider this relaxation procedure as an option when detoxing. Prepare yourself for the Peaceful Place Relaxation coming next:

As before, relax yourself. Close your eyes. Very slowly take three deep breaths. Slowly count backwards from ten to one. Imagine yourself in your very restful place – a favourite room, at the seaside, in the mountains, on a sailing boat or in a garden.

> Wherever is your favourite place, go there now. You can make-believe the place if you like. Remember that your body cannot tell the difference between real or vividly imagined experiences. Let yourself enjoy the place you have chosen. When your thoughts wander, just refocus, and when your thoughts wander again, just refocus again, and again as necessary.

From within the state of relaxation, a place ripe for contemplation, bring to mind the first member of your old team, one you now wish to detox and eliminate. Sense the presence of the player in yourself. Thank the team player for coming forward.

Now from your state of stillness begin a search. The search is intended to bring forward the team player in the form of a shape, or an object, or perhaps a feeling; to scan the misty recesses of your inner mind; to scour the darker chambers that all lead off from the brightly lit changing room.

Perform this search in a respectful, loving, fair, but firm way. In your imagination seek out the sensations, imagined though they may be, and a sense of the feelings, memories, words and phrases that are allied to the team member, and bring them forward in the form of a shape, an object or a feeling. The shape or the object may be indistinct. It may appear in shadow. No matter. What is important is that you have a sense of something coming forward.

Having brought forward a sense of the team member, your next task is to eliminate it in any way you choose, just as Dorothy liquidated the Wicked Witch of the West in the film *The Wizard of Oz*. When the sense is in the form of a feeling or a sound, bring it forward and place it in a box. Then notice what the box is made of.

How you choose to destroy the shape, object or the box is entirely up to you. Be surprised. A way of destroying the shape will just pop up from the inner mind. Whatever you do, ensure the shape, object or the box is destroyed completely and absolutely, leaving no trace, no trace whatsoever.

What follows are some case-stories to illustrate just how powerful visualizing elimination and destruction can be in beginning to lighten up and let go.

- Insecurity came forward as a prism, a triangle that was held within the body of my client, Jane. The base resided in her waist, and tapered to a point around her heart and throat. It was made of a dull gold resembling the colour of bronze. Jane reported that she wanted to shoot it out. In response, she came forward with a picture of herself pulling the prism back on a strong bow, pulling it back and then ... letting it go ... watching it fly out to the light as a rocket going into space. Out of sight. Out of mind. She reported its base as flooded with the light, and then it was gone.

- In Michelle's mind, Dependence on cigarettes came forward as a long, cylindrical shape made of white marble. An army of angels picked the marble shape up and stood it amongst the trees. The angels proceeded to push the shape down into the ground until it was completely buried.

- Susan sensed an ongoing Battle amongst her team, blocking her inner light. She described a boulder, rough and heavy. She sensed something was needed to crack it. Fierce winds and torrential rains made little impact in wearing it down. The 'heavy stuff', as she described them, did not 'crack it'. Eventual success came with Love to transform the boulder into a habitable place, a more living thing, allowing species that could survive to live on the surface.

- Righteous Anger was reluctant to go, and expressed itself as a bread roll. Sarah's inner mind revealed compassion for it, for she said it had a brain. The bread roll was encased in a housing, upon which was written 'Press this Button Now and Destroy the Bread Roll'. Sarah followed the instruction, and reported that the anger was now a distant memory.

A team member who identified herself as Ratty, came forward determined to stay. Moments later, mollified by Love, she just melted away, and was gone.

 Karen reported that Guilt had been hammered into her, and that she sensed GUILT written in big letters across her brain. Feeling guilt stopped her enjoying her successes and contributed to her experience of 'spiralling levels of stress'. Stress sparked off a muscle problem which had been diagnosed as Repetitive Strain Injury (RSI). Karen consciously conceded that she had *learned* to feel guilt. Just as one can *learn* a good habit, one can *unlearn* a bad habit, like stopping smoking – like feeling guilt. This is what happened. Guilt stepped forward as one chapter in a Book of Knowledge. I requested that the inner mind turn to the pages where this knowledge was written. It transpired that the 'problem pages' were edged in black. I asked the Book of Knowledge whether it would agree for the 'problem pages' to be very carefully and very respectfully removed and solemnly destroyed. The book agreed and very carefully and very respectfully tore them out and set fire to the pages.

Guilt had agreed to go. Then, in the process of elimination, Guilt almost disappeared – but not quite: a fraction of the shape or form remained there to drive Karen to distraction! When this happens, help is generally at hand.

And so it was that the pages burned with one small exception. One little bit of charred paper persistently returned. Karen summoned a wise being to help her. An angel came forward and poured petrol over the resistant piece of paper and held it down whilst it burnt. When only dust and embers remained, a travelling wind swept up the ash and the dust, transporting it far, far away, out of sight, out of mind. 'Yes. Done it,' reported inner mind. Karen breathed a sigh of relief.

Some shapes and forms are just so mighty, and so entrenched, that when it comes to fighting the good fight you just have to bring in reinforcements, in the form of beings or equipment, to make any impact at all.

When Rogue Players Strike Back

Now and again, when team members have agreed to go in principle, they may nonetheless return again, and again, whenever the appropriate signals provocatively trigger their re-emergence. Anger falls into this camp. So too do Negativity, Fear, Rejection and Guilt. Just when you thought you had conquered your biggest emotional challenge, it is back full in your face. Only this time, perhaps you noticed more about the train of events that led up to the response. Perhaps you were more conscious? Your previous session, although it was not the end of the story, may well have given you an increased sense of clarity and understanding – understanding of the driving forces behind the anger, the triggers. And perhaps now you can begin to engage in dialogue with those trigger-happy players who shoot from the hip. Session by session, you will dilute the strength of the toxic reaction until you are fully conscious of a pattern of behaviour over which, previously, you had apparently had no control. You will know your 'rogue', and increasingly have team members in place who remind you of your other choices, ways of being lighter about the same business that used to blow you out.

 In Karen's case, Guilt returned. On request again, Guilt agreed to go, acknowledging she was long since made redundant. The inner mind gathered the team member up in 'an embrace', such that Guilt transformed into a black fluffy cloud. The inner mind then proceeded to blow the cloud over the hill with love and understanding.

Guilt did not return. Perhaps the word 'embrace' sheds light on the reason why Guilt stepped down from Karen's team. When you *embrace* you hold, you acknowledge, you contain without judgement. Once accepted and understood, Guilt felt lighter, and floated away ... (feeling loved ... feeling understood) ... over the hill and far away ... Karen reported feeling brighter. Three days later she reported feeling more loving, more accepting and more forgiving.

Detox is a process that can enable you to be more present, more honest and more truthful and understanding of yourself and of the workings of your inner mind. The less you resist something, the less it will persist. Being aware, being honest, being truthful to yourself is crucial to your success. Having observed a feeling, an emotion, a reaction – call it what you will – be with it, and detox!

For example, let us say that a feeling of Judgement (about something, or someone) speaks within you. Acknowledge it. Close your eyes. Dive into the pool of light within yourself. Be there. Sense yourself sensing and searching for each and every word of Judgement, and particularly the judgemental thought just passed. Seek out each and every trace of Judgement, and bring it forward in the form of a shape, or an object, or a phrase. Then eliminate the form, destroying it in the first way that comes to mind. When done, sense the difference.

In the same way, say a feeling of Sadness (about something, or someone) stirs within you. Acknowledge it. Close your eyes. Dive into the pool of light within you. Be there. Sense yourself sensing and searching for each and every feeling of Sadness associated with that thought, situation or circumstance. Seek out each and every trace of Sadness, and bring it forward in the form of a shape, or an object, or a phrase. Choose to destroy or release the presenting form. Sometimes a peace offering may present itself, or indeed a gift, perhaps in the form of a bird. Release it. Let it fly away and leave you. Observe it flying higher and higher, beyond the clouds, and away. When done, smile at the difference.

And in the same way, say a feeling of Jealousy stirs within you. Acknowledge the feeling. Notice where it is held within the body. Close your eyes. Dive into the pool of light within you. Be there. Sense yourself sensing and searching for each and every feeling of Jealousy, and particularly the most recent sensation of Jealousy. Seek out each and every trace of Jealousy, and bring it forward in the form of a shape, or an object, or a phrase. Then eliminate the form, destroying it in any way that comes to mind. When done, sense the difference.

You can do this with Pain, with Anger, with Worry, over and over, time and again. We think the same thoughts over and over. Now choose to replace some of those redundant thoughts with ones that detox and clear over and over, time and again.

The more you deliberately detox, the more dilute will become recurring themes and emotions. The detox process will weaken those emotions that have denied you your inner glow; emotions that, by their strength, seek to control – to pollute, to poison and to damage and undermine. Emotions that seriously damage your health and your emotional wealth.

The detox process will help you cleanse your sense of self and your sense of soul. Just as you wash and bathe each day, so it is recommended to cleanse your inner mind. And, with practice, it will take as little time as it takes to clean your teeth! The more and more you detox, what once was the mind-field will increasingly become a field furrowed and fertile for dreams and fresh sensations of self to flourish.

Getting Help to Polish the Jewels

As Karen did, you may also request the help of wise beings, human or otherwise, and you can bring on board equipment, tools and services to work towards your ultimate success. We may sometimes be down, but our championing team is not out!

All you have to do is to ask, and help will be there to minister to your requirements. Invite a friend, or a friendly relative, one whose wisdom you trust and whose love and integrity you respect, into your inner mind. The friend or relative may be one who has died, and lives on in your heart.

Alternatively, and for those readers who feel that no family member or friend fits the description, you may invite a mystical being, an imaginary being, a being from a film or a television programme, or from a painting that you have seen in an art gallery. Again, the 'being' you choose should be one accustomed to championing success against amazing odds. An angel is an increasingly popular and well-practised form to fight your good fight. It might be a stereotypical angelic entity, possessing the archetypal characteristics of angels, such as luminosity, purity and strength. Alternatively, it might be a particular angel, such as one of the three archangels mentioned in the Bible: the immeasurably strong warrior Michael, or the enlightening messenger Gabriel, or the healer Raphael. (David Connolly's book *In Search of Angels* is a good place to look if you wish to expand your ideas of angels.) You just have to know that this 'being' is on your team, right by your side, and willing to work against seemingly tough odds to win out for your positive and advantageous benefit.

Now that your imaginary being is at your side, consult with him or her on the best way to eliminate and destroy the shape or form before you. Set about the task together. Success is so often assured when a familiar friend is at your side. Together, each of you can achieve more.

Occasionally, the imaginary being may suggest that you need more help, in which case you may bring your whole family into the frame, or a whole fraternity of friends. Imagine that a numberless army of imaginary beings could be put at your disposal to face strong resistance if necessary. Trust that whatever it takes can be supplied to you, provided it is for your positive and advantageous benefit.

As you've discovered, shapes and objects can be enormous and made of seemingly indestructible materials. Or they can be so minute and lightweight and yet as provocative as a gadfly that they make very difficult targets to hit. You may find that other shapes, in any of many sizes, can be destroyed with apparent ease, except for a fragment: that fragment may seek to frustrate before your inner eyes – disappearing and then reappearing as if dancing – seemingly defying destruction. This situation can be maddeningly frustrating.

When fragments and leftover bits of shapes and forms present themselves as targets that are adept at dodging destruction, you can bring on board your imaginary being. Angels are highly skilled at netting provocative and precocious will-o'-the-wisp fragments that seem to elude your inner grasp. Your family, friends and imaginary beings will have other ideas that could be helpful. Listen, and then together take action. And, when the elimination is completely over and done with, thank your imaginary being wholeheartedly for his or her (or its) assistance and support, then let the being go. You can be sure that when called to assist you again such beings will be available and ready and willing to assist your team. Just ask!

 To Edwina came help in the form of a spiritual horse. The horse bore the promise that its abilities and talents were unstoppable. A sense of its gentleness and strength filled Edwina's mind, such that the mere presence of the helper dissolved her memory of a 'black shape'.

In your imagination you can do or be whatever you wish to do or be. Hence, at your disposal is a sophisticated range of state-of-the-art industrial equipment. This can include cranes and lifting equipment, crushing equipment, water hoses, drainage equipment, and an arsenal of furnaces. If you can think of the item then you can rely on its being in stock, and delivered – in a twinkling of your inner eye. Your inner mind can truly luxuriate in the sense of having a limitless budget to spend on kicking the habits – sometimes of a lifetime.

Justin experienced severe congestion that disturbed his focus and concentration. He reported the ease with which grit could get into his mind and clog it up. This state of events was created by the team member Dirt. Dirt presented himself as if a tanker had run aground and spilled its contents onto a beach. Inner mind then ran aground in a mind-field of silt which was now being stirred up at the bottom of the sea. The black silt was a potent and poisonous mix that blocked our hero's reaching the clear waters of clarity and focus. Inner mind allocated a limitless budget, bringing on board state-of-the-art dredging and drainage equipment, and helpers in the form of technicians and specialists. Inner mind reported that his team were dredging the sea bed, and as he spoke, were sweeping the beach. All the dangerous fish and poisonous elements were being captured and removed. The water was becoming increasingly pure as the black silt dissipated. As the last particles of black silt drained away he felt himself rolling in the warmer, clearer waters, celebrating his success. The resisting Dirt had gone.

To conclude, Justin invited first Focus, then Clarity forward to advance suggestions that would allow him to think increasingly clearly. The visualization of the clearing had reinstated the possibility of their presence on Justin's inner team.

Like Karen, who was disposed to feeling Guilt, Justin in a follow-up detox session experienced further resistance. Resistance came forward as a 'many-headed monster', a gargoyle of sorts. Again, he brought forward the team of technicians and experts who had previously helped him, and who now co-operated in slaying the monster, and burying it deep in the earth. Resistance did prove to be a powerful rogue player. Amidst the earth, Resistance writhed and twitched, until finally with perseverance on behalf of the team, the rogue was dissolved and turned to dust. It was a challenging visualization, during which an inner demon was surely put to rest. Immediately Justin reported feeling brighter, fresher and freer. He had liberated himself.

As you become more aware of the divisive players in your team, such as Resistance, the rest of the team are much less likely to be as imprisoned by them. This is because you now know that you have access to your own inner wisdom, your own inner mind to negotiate a more level emotional playing field.

 Catherine's case involved the rogue player, Low Self-worth. The team member came forward for elimination as a square-shaped box made of cardboard. Inner mind promptly flattened it and posted it to Tibet. Resistance rallied immediately, saying that she would intercept the post and send it back. The tit-for-tat was promptly settled by Wisdom, who promised to accompany the package and 'sort everything out at the other end'. Inner mind observed the postman come to collect the post. The package was placed in a hessian bag, and delivered into the mail van en route to Tibet – a land far, far, away – out of sight and out of mind. Wisdom, as good as her word, accompanied the package all the way to Tibet. Catherine then invited a player called Positive Belief forward, to share a new and empowering set of beliefs – ones that would herald and champion her success.

Here are some more case-stories:

- Frustration presented herself as a big, bloated balloon with arms and legs. Karen burst the balloon, and then set fire to it. The resulting sticky mess was gathered up by a wise being who flew away with it.

- Scared ventured forward as a black, hard and shiny square shape. Initially the corners were softened by the weathering effects of the wind, such that the black, hard, shiny square shape became smaller and smaller until no trace was left. No trace whatsoever.

- Sadness felt very let down and came forward with a splash, a round splash of bright red paint, which Nicole's inner mind hosed down. The pressure of the water diluted the depth of colour until finally the splash had been completely washed away.

- For Tina, Guilt came forward as a snake. Inner mind commanded the snake to go for ever. Inner mind told it straight: 'I don't want to see you anymore. I know what you've done.' The snake left. Gone.

- Fear of heights produced a chequered handkerchief tied in knots. Kate's inner mind unceremoniously trod on it, and proceeded to drop it over a precipice, at the top of which she was standing, at a safe distance from the edge – looking down, and feeling fine.

An undesired Habit stepped out as a strange little character, holding a string bag full of things. Inner mind unceremoniously took him to outer space and blew him up. The man was gone. Eliminated completely and absolutely.

John reported feeling Blocked creatively. The sense of being blocked resided in a knot at the back of his neck. Inner mind untied the knot to open up creativity.

Sweet Tooth came forward as a jelly bean. Inner mind poured boiling water over the jelly bean causing it to melt, and promptly poured it down the sink.

Jane had decided to limit herself to two glasses of wine a night in a concerted effort to let go of excess weight. Temptation to drink in excess of this took the guise of a curvaceous shape made of a gelatinous substance. In this case inner mind pushed it out of the owner's body as superfluous waste, and it just vanished.

Cassandra's sensory acuity with regard to her joint disease was text-book perfect, and her courage and commitment to containing the condition a triumph of mind over matter on her part. During one session, a sense of Muddle emerged in the middle of a dialogue. Inner mind gathered together every feeling and every sensation of Muddle, every muddled thought, sentence, phrase and word, and brought Muddle forward as a black ball of string. Inner mind committed to burn the string. To prepare, she set about unravelling the Muddle, and having presented the former ball as a long and continuous strand of string, set fire to one end with a taper. The flame steadily moved along, progressively burning up the former Muddle, and discarding the ash onto the floor. As the threads disintegrated, the word 'pivot' popped into her mind. Pivot presented an image of two balls, balanced; one large, one small. The larger of the two was balanced upon the smaller. Balance acknowledged the world in balance, in particular her world in balance, and the balls (of her joints) as existing in perfect balance – rolling perfectly along together. Clarity and Understanding followed, manifesting not as words, but as a crystal ball, a perfectly round crystal ball. Freshly positioned, these three jewels sparkled creatively, creating a team steadily being coached towards personal growth, a team focused on playing full-out to keep Cassandra in the best position to participate fully in her life.

Elimination Versus Release

The ultimate aim is to remove negative team members from your inner mind – players who are not working fully for your positive and advantageous benefit. As you've discovered, the detox process encourages the negative aspect to come forward in the form of a shape. The inner mind is then asked to destroy the shape in any way it chooses, and to ensure there is no trace of that shape whatsoever in the inner mind. So far so good! Unless the shape that is presented is a bird, a butterfly, a flower, or some other living being which you do not feel comfortable about destroying in the literal sense of the word. On one occasion, a profound sense of Sadness swam from the depths of Ben's inner mind in the shape of a whale.

In such circumstances, I recommend not destruction but release from the inner mind. Once released, the former team member (in the form of a shape), may be jettisoned into the ocean, or to an island far away, released into a sanctuary or a safe and secure haven from where it will never need to escape. The whale was released into a calm, azure blue ocean, and swam away. This allows for the 'shape' to be spared from destruction. The shape is effectively exiled to a place 'out of sight, out of mind'. This is necessary and essential for the process to be completed. Do not, however, shy away from 'destroying' beings if your inner mind chooses this option. The choice of elimination versus release is there simply to offer choice in case you are disinclined to pass a sentence of obliteration on a living creature, even if that living creature is only in your mind. Trust your inner mind to make the correct decision and act accordingly.

 Rooted within Roberta was a knot of Nervousness. Inner mind did not wish to destroy it. It agreed, however, to be transplanted, with the entire root ball intact, into a very special forest, out of sight and out of Roberta's inner mind.

Destruction: Sensing is as Good as Seeing

You may discover that you have an ability to see pictures in the inner mind with a clarity and vividness as real as if you had your eyes open. Furthermore, you may find that you are able to 'run movies' in your mind. In particular, you may be able to 'see' and 'view' the process of elimination or release. You may find you have an acute sense of the setting, the props and the supporting players that contribute to the action of ridding yourself of a rogue player.

On the other hand, you may find that you have only a dim and sketchy view of what may be happening in shadow and half-shadow. Occasionally, perhaps, you may sense a 'window opening' to provide a clearer sight of what is happening during the elimination process. You may experience feelings of release and a sense of lightness, peace and contentment.

Again, you may find that you have only a non-sensory awareness. You may see nothing in your mind's eye, and only 'sense' what is happening. Occasionally you may experience change from a patchy or plain darkness to a sense of light or lightness. Occasionally, too, swirling colours may envelop you.

So whether you see, sense or feel sensations within yourself, trust that your particular response to the detox is special and appropriate for you.

Each detox session will be pertinent at the time, and as you become ever more familiar with detoxing you will achieve ever more beneficial and advantageous results.

Varieties of the Elimination Process

As you have discovered, negative and unsupportive players are requested to present themselves in the form of a shape. The shapes and objects that come forward for elimination and release will continue to create interest, surprise and perhaps even entertainment. When the rogue player presents herself as a shape you can expect any one of many possible geometric shapes to appear in your inner mind. Whether it be a square, circle or rectangle, always investigate or sense what it is made of. Again the range of materials is as wide as can be. It could be metal, wood, plastic, even smoke. These shapes can disappear in one hearty great puff!

After imagining the team member as a shape, there follows the elimination process itself. You will find that by far the most common way of destroying or eliminating a shape is to burn it. When the fire is out and the embers are cool, a gentle breeze may be commanded to carry the ashes and the dust far, far away. Out of sight and out of mind!

Here are some examples and a brief mention of what happened during the elimination process and destruction process:

A circle made of stainless steel:
  placed in a steel furnace and melted down.

A pyramid made of bricks:
  smashed into tiny pieces, crushed to a powder and then blown away into the breeze.

A pyramid made of plastic:
  trodden on, flattened and finally burned away.

A square made of people:
  pushed away into the infinite distance, where it is still receding.

Triangles made of wood:

broken into pieces and kicked miles away; another was burnt.

A triangle made of metal:

bent and buckled out of shape, and then melted down.

A triangle made of green plastic with a bevelled edge:

melted down and drained away.

A cylinder made of aluminium:

smashed and the pieces swept away.

A circle made of stone:

blown up and the fragments spread far and wide.

Then there are objects that come forward:

A wall made of bricks:

bull-dozed flat.

A ball made of rubber:

blown up leaving no trace at all.

A ball made of plastic:

stuck with a pin and shrivelled up.

A plate:

smashed.

A black bowl:

exploded by a beam of light.

An orange-juice carton:

smashed with a rolling pin.

A candle:

burnt down and the residual wax swept into a rubbish bin.

A red balloon:

popped.

A brown leather shoe:

ended life on a bonfire.

A wiggly, wavy string of sausages:

placed in a pot and cooked.

Bear in mind that strong and destructive tools or techniques can also be creative. In the literal realm, we find that out of a furnace, out of the intense fire at its heart, we can manifest a thing of beauty, such as a sculpture moulded in clay. In the magical realm of imagery, one client found that a hammer, placed into a furnace to be melted down and destroyed, was replaced – after the destruction was complete – with a complete vase of flowers. This was a movement towards the person's embracing her true expression, her true colours.

11

Freeing Yourself from a Life Sentence

Perhaps you have a sense of someone speaking over your shoulder. The voice judges, criticizes, exercises its opinion without being asked. A sentence or phrase will form in your thoughts. The sentence speaks its mind. It may sound like the voice of a back-seat driver. The voice will stop you in the middle of play. It will halt you in your confident tracks. It will proclaim sentence, time and time again. The voice will generally succeed in interrupting your present Game of Life.

- ■ 'If I speak intelligently, I'll come across as a know-it-all.' The holder of this life sentence believed she was stupid.

- ■ 'To speak about oneself and one's achievements is precocious and boastful.' The holder of this life sentence had difficulty in recognizing and remembering the great and wonderful achievements in her life. Hence she lacked confidence, self-esteem and self-worth, having 'erased' her memories of the great and the good things that she had done.

- ■ 'You've never done anything creative in your life.' The holder of this belief did not recognize the wonderfully creative things he did.

- ■ 'I'm not allowed to make mistakes. I have to do everything right.' This sentence contributed to the owner's experiencing extreme feelings of shyness, self-consciousness, and a sense of always feeling uncomfortable.

- 'That's crap.' This sentence stopped the holder getting past the first post.

- 'It won't be good enough' and 'It won't be on time.' These sentences were a cause of constant worry.

- 'When I open my mouth, frogs pop out instead of pearls.' This sentence disallowed the prisoner from feeling relaxed with herself, and locked her into a belief that whatever she did would not be good enough.

- 'You stammer, you do' were words uttered to a contemporary, as 'just something to say'. They were said at a vulnerable moment when my client was open to receiving them. 'You stammer, you do': the receiver of that sentence, until then, had spoken lucidly and fluently. Gradually the youngster 'developed' a stammer, having been open to suggestion at the time, and having by chance been confronted by his worst fear. It become a self-fulfilling prophecy. Some 20 years later the young man came to my practice to discover when the seed of the stammer first rooted and to begin to free himself from that life sentence.

You may benefit from taking time out to reflect on any life sentences you are now serving.

Whatever this sentence may be, take action to eliminate it now. Remember to capture, or to get a sense of, the sentence when next the voice speaks. Granted this is difficult, as the voice can speak in a flash and be gone. Sometimes remembering the sentence can be as seemingly challenging as remembering your dreams. In the same way as you resolve to remember your dreams, resolve to reclaim the sentence. Persevere until you recognize the sentence in your still mind's eye.

Once captured, sense the sentence written in front of you. Take a pair of scissors or some shears. Become aware of yourself cutting the sentence up into pieces, and placing the words comprising the sentence into a box. Notice what the box is made of. Then destroy the box, in the same imaginative and surprising way that you have become used to destroying shapes and other objects. If you like, blow the sentence up in the back seat of a car!

Do this time and again until the sentence loses its hold, until the chains of influence cease to bind you. Get on with the Game of Life.

Another way of disposing of life sentences is to put all of the words inside a balloon. Once the balloon is sky high, pop it. As you become increasingly adept at ridding yourself of life sentences, you will devise and develop many other creative ways of disposing of them. If a technique works for you, nothing is too ridiculous or outrageous. Just blast the past!

Some life sentences may be more difficult to shift than others. You may have a sense of them, and yet be unable to trace them. The young man who had accepted the 'sentence' of his classmate completely and absolutely knew that before the age of 11 he did not stammer. He also knew that the stammer kicked in around age 11, and had gradually taken hold and somehow evolved, such that with practice it had become a part of himself. In spite of this knowledge he was not able to grasp the exact words of the sentence. In this kind of case, one-to-one work with a qualified hypnotherapist practising interactive hypnotherapy may help you locate the sentence accurately and quickly, about which more information is given in the next chapter. You could regard yourself as bringing in a private investigator to help you with your enquiries.

Once you know where the sentence is originating and the form of words the sentence comprises, you are well on your way to claiming your freedom. Knowledge of the words brings clarity, understanding and healing. So you are released and on your way to liberating yourself completely.

I must stress the importance of accessing the sentence at the root. At the root lies the cause of a tendency to think in a certain way or to behave in a certain way. In the root of the sentence lies the route to making known what is unknown. It is essential to access the sentence and pull it out by its roots.

Take a break for a few moments, and imagine yourself looking out onto a garden. It can be a garden you know, or indeed an imaginary garden. There in the garden you notice several dandelion flowers sprouting through in the midst of your finer exhibits. You have a choice. You can remove the leaf-tops of the dandelions, suggesting that the dandelions have been removed completely. If you do this they will of course sprout again. Or you can take a trowel and remove the dandelions at the root. When you access the root you are then in a position to remove the root-cause of the problem, the dandelion, and so the source of the sentence. Apologies to dandelions!

This is what you must seek to do to ensure the detox is lasting and long-term. (Please, no letters replying that dandelions have a lot of seeds!)

The Dustbin Collectors

Following the destruction and elimination process, you are advised to check that there is no trace, none whatsoever, of the offending shape. Occasionally, fragments and pieces have already been consigned to a dustbin. What should you then do with the rubbish bin? On some occasions you may wish to go so far as to have the bin removed. Having sensed this is the best course of action, begin to sense a dustcart promptly pulling up alongside you. Two people descend from the truck. Carefully they lift the rubbish bin into the truck, in its entirety – carefully avoiding spilling anything! They then climb back into the truck and drive away. Observe them driving away, far away – out of sight, out of mind!

Buried Treasure

Within you lies a wealth of buried treasure. Divine virtues, your inner treasures, are those qualities that are universally recognized as supremely good. The list that follows has been made available with the kind permission of The Brahma Kumaris World Spiritual University (a non-governmental organization in consultative status with the United Nations Economic and Social Council and UNICEF). Think of it as a treasure chest of invaluable words that can name and call forth good players to have in your inner team, and connotations out of which you can build a release from your life sentence.

Accuracy	Fearlessness
Loyalty	Serenity
Benevolence	Flexibility
Maturity	Simplicity
Carefree	Generosity
Mercy	Stability
Cheerfulness	Gentleness
Cleanliness	Surrender
Patience	Happiness
Contentment	Sweetness
Peacefulness	Honesty
Co-operation	Tirelessness
Purity	Humility
Courage	Tolerance
Respect	Trustworthiness
Detachment	Truthfulness
Responsibility	Lightness
Determination	Unity
Discipline	Love
Self-confidence	Wisdom

You can start digging right now!

12

Doing the Mind Detox

The detox process is a way of helping you to help yourself. It is an investment of time. Remember, you can do anything, if you put your mind to it!

Please read and reread these sections after your first few detox sessions. It is a challenge to remember all the helpful signposts in one go, and you may find it insightful to revisit them.

Putting the Team to Work

The practicalities of building a supportive inner team will depend on what you feel comfortable with. As I mentioned at the outset, you may wish to have a pencil and paper at your side to keep a record of each session's coaching and team progress. I also suggest visual cues, of which I shall say more later in this chapter. You may choose to follow the guided exercise that is included on Side B of the audio cassette tape, available as a stand-alone companion to this book. Furthermore, you may tape-record your sessions, speaking aloud the stages of the detox process.

At this early stage do jot down brief notes onto paper. There are two reasons for doing this. Firstly, when you look back over several sessions, it will give you a sense of progress: you will see more clearly where you are coming from, where you have been to, and where you are heading towards as you travel along your own personal Yellow Brick Road.

Secondly, recording your session in progress will help to lock you into the detox process and help to prevent your mind from wandering off in random directions: it will help you build up the momentum and commitment to keep moving towards the desired change.

Be Clear About Your Outcome

To start with, have a clear idea of what problem you want to deal with. The problem could be simple or complex, but it helps to find a succinct way to articulate it. Pin it down in one short sentence. If you expand it into a longer description, then you will make it diffuse and that will deflect the power of the detox method away from your target. Ideally, get a single word or phrase that sums up in essence what the problem is: Smoking, Weight Loss, Confidence Building or some such.

State your intended change to your inner mind in the following manner. Preferably address yourself in the third person, referring to yourself by your actual name rather than as 'you' or 'me'. Suppose that the problem you want to deal with is low self-confidence: then the statement to the inner mind would commence as follows. 'Inner mind, what is the reason for <your name>'s lacking confidence?'

Generally a word will come forward. The word invoked corresponds to the name of a member of your inner team. This team member, in some imagined form, will provide a focus for communication.

If you find words and phrases coming up and you are not happy about dealing with them on your own, then please do consider seeking help from a professional, practising interactive hypnotherapy. If you choose this option, it is to your advantage that you fully participate in any such therapy, which means to say you will be speaking (more than likely aloud) during the process of therapy. Your participation and personal say in your desired change enhances the potency of the therapy and your sense of self-empowerment. And again, as with Mind Detoxing, you will be accessing your own inner wisdom and therefore will accelerate the experience of clarity, understanding, release and transformation. This book is not a replacement for therapy; it is an adjunct to enable you to do work on your own and perhaps also to supplement therapy where appropriate. Julie Soskin in her channelled work, *Alignment to Light*, touches on the importance of the personal process:

> Many of you will welcome an opportunity to enter into a dialogue with your own inner knowledge … Many of you will realise that you do not need others to tell you what you know within your heart.

This process offers you the opportunity to step within, to access and accept your own power. She continues:

> You can and you will be complete within yourselves, by knowing and touching your Light force within … Of course, we are not saying to you that you do not need friends and advisers. Listen to your friends, but make up your own mind.

As a practical measure to help motivate you, you may create a poster, offering a visual suggestion of your 'field of dreams' – a field upon which your new team members are about to set foot. Identify the players whom you wish to eliminate, writing their names in positions on the field. Key saboteurs may be positioned centre-field, with lesser rogues to be placed mid-field and on the boundaries of the field. If you've chosen to pair saboteurs with enlightened substitutes, then write their names alongside, again positioning your strongest allies alongside your stronger saboteurs. Alternatively, when you do have the time, you may make an 'advent calendar' of sorts, with your rogues on the facing flaps. Each day as a new and fresh substitute takes over, open the window to acknowledge their arrival, and tear away the redundant label. Visual triggers will remind you to practise and strengthen your positive players.

Initially, you will find yourself diving into and out of the contemplative state following each question and response. You will be 'surfacing' time and again, to note down a player, or to record their suggestions as you choose. As you become familiar with the structure of the process you will be able to stay within the contemplative state for longer, and eventually complete more and more of the dialogue exchange until eventually you emerge only when the detox is completely done.

Two analogies come to mind. Those readers who drive may recall their experience of learning to drive. During the initial lessons you consciously handled all of the operations necessary to drive – the steering, positioning the hands at ten-to-two, flicking the indicators, changing gear, and remembering to look in the rear- and side-view mirrors virtually simultaneously. At least, this is how it felt. Those of you to whom this experience applies may, some time this week, be curious to notice that you've arrived at B, with almost no memory of all the operations and actions taken from A. Now you drive with a sense of unconscious competence. In other words, your inner mind takes over, having installed within a winning team of players who know how to drive competently with an inner eye open for both your Safety and your intended Route. Inner teams who experience any sense of players called Rage or Anger, when driving, should choose to eliminate them as you course the road to inner success.

The second analogy is suggested by learning any kind of bodily exercise from a book – yoga, for instance. You may find yourself going backwards and forwards to the book in mid-detox to remind yourself what to do next. Your reaction is understandable. Again, study the method and stay with it, because you may be surprised that the work is done in some ways intuitively behind the scenes. Behind your closed, but all-seeing and sensing, eyes you will sense a change in yourself. You may observe the presence of a colour swirling before you or an adjustment in your posture. It is not unusual for a person to report a sense of patchy or plain blackness at the start and to enter into a state of lightness or swirling colour at the end. Consider these signs as positive and progressive, and indications that you are moving forward. Just by beginning to exercise the mind, you will induce positive changes. Your focus and concentration will improve. You will experience an increasing sense of peace and wellbeing: just by beginning to switch off some of the internal babble, you will realize more of your latent energy.

The words that come forward from within your inner mind may well be quite different to the words listed in each of the case examples that follow. These words are included only to illustrate the power of the play of words to arrest your habit, and to transform behaviour. Moreover, they can illustrate how you view your life, and your inner ability to take control of it through the power of thought, and the composition of words that go to make up your thoughts. Sometimes, if you change the words, you can transform their inner effect on you.

You may find that a word will present itself to you, perhaps a spoken word, or a word that you see in your mind's eye, or just the sense of a word. Repeat it to yourself three times to fix it in your memory. As you open your eyes, just bring that word forward. The word may suggest an issue that, consciously or unconsciously, you want to address. It may be a word that relates only symbolically to the issue. As you will in time discover, your inner mind has a profoundly inventive capacity to devise far-fetched or even bizarre symbols for things. Do not let that trouble you. Be tolerant and allow your unconscious mind to employ the symbols that it is most comfortable with.

It is in the fleeting instant that you can catch a feeling, a thought, a sensation and ask yourself what it signifies. We may experience one strong feeling – positive or negative – or we may experience mixed feelings that encompass both positive and negative dimensions.

Managing Your Inner Team

The next step in your journey toward detoxing your mind is to find the team member that is responsible for whatever problem, challenge or difficulty you are facing. Usually, it is hidden in your inner mind, where it works invisibly, weaving its influence without your being aware of it. You can change it only by bringing it out into the light, so that you can communicate with it.

Throughout the detox method, always proceed by 'negotiating' with your inner mind. Formulate what you want to say slowly and carefully, and then speak the words in your head or aloud, if you've chosen to tape-record the session.

It is fair to say that during the early days of your detox, and until you become practised, you will tend to wander off and lose track of the conversation. Random thoughts may just pop in – things you have to do, things you've told yourself to remember, and so forth. When this happens just gently steer yourself back on course, and if necessary begin the dialogue again. Anyone who has set off on a course of learning meditation will be well aware of how difficult it can be at first to stay with the word that may have been assigned, or with the regular ebb and flow of the breath. Meditation teachers will counsel that the natural tendency of the mind, when one initially seeks to take action to quieten or control it, is for the mind to resist, to come up with objections, and to side-track. The same is true with regard to detoxing the mind. Stay with the process. Bear with it, be patient and practise.

The detox process is not about bullying. Detox is a dialogue to enable you to be more present, more honest, truthful and understanding of yourself and of the workings of your inner mind. I would counsel respectful communication, and deference to the decisions of the inner mind, in order to promote continuation of the dialogue. You do not, however, have to accept a decision without its being qualified in full, so as to bring out the precise meaning, and having ensured that principled, supportive and balanced suggestions are in place. You have available to you assistance in the form of other players: Creative and Wise, who were mentioned earlier. You may invite them to come forward with suggestions to free up a stuck situation. You may also request the help of wise beings, human or otherwise, and you can bring on board equipment, tools and services to work towards your ultimate success. We may sometimes be down, but our championing team is not out!

When you are more *aware* of the divisive players in your team, then the rest of the team is much less likely to be as imprisoned by them, because now you know that you have access to your own inner wisdom – to negotiate a more level playing field.

Thoughts and Ideas – How They Come Forward

The detox process may be compared to the exchange one might share in a word-association game. For instance: I say one word, and then you immediately respond with another word without thinking about it at all. You just say whatever word first pops into your mind, with no consideration to revising it or opting for a second word following close behind. So it is important that you go forward into the dialogue with the words as they present themselves, however odd, curious, extravagant or exotic they appear to be. You might find yourself thinking, 'No, that can't be right – it makes no sense to me!', but do trust whatever your mind first produces. As Chögyam Trungpa said, 'First thought, best thought!' The inner mind has its own reasons for saying what it does, and you must wait patiently for the true, underlying meaning to become clearer to you, as it eventually will. Coach your inner team on the basis that all words are worthy and relevant. As you become more practised in the art of detoxing you will find that you can run through a session or a booster session in five minutes or so. You will then be ready and raring to face the world with confidence, standing forward in strength, truth, clarity, and more fully self-expressed.

Some words that present themselves may seem so exotic that they transport you instantaneously into a reverie of sheer delight. Some may trigger memories, sights, sounds and smells. As I previously shared, the mind will try to take many meandering paths from the straight and narrow. Gently rein in the fantasy and remind your inner team of the task in hand. Continue the mindful dialogue and listen to and acknowledge the inner response with kindness and respect. Also notice how your body moves and shifts in response to the inner dialogue, how the colours on your inner landscape change.

Another coaching point worth mentioning here is that words do come forward as nouns, verbs and adjectives. These designations may appear inconsistent. It is true, however, that inner mind does tend to opt for the shortest form of a word, irrespective of what part of speech it is. For instance, it chooses Courage rather than Courageous, and Brave rather than Bravery.

Negative Labels, Positive Players

Team players will on occasion come forward with strong and severe-sounding names. A player that comes forward, say, with the name War should not immediately be assumed to be necessarily negative. Players who sound aggressive may well hold a positive intention – say, to ensure you are dynamic, forceful and strong. They are there to insist that you take action, rather than succumbing to complacency and indolence.

Positive Labels, Negative Players

A seemingly complex situation arises when you are negotiating with a team member who, on the face of it, you would deem positive, and yet is behaving in a way that is limiting your sense of freedom and liberation. One example is a player with an overly protective nature, which works to keep you as far away as possible from potential anxiety and potentially anxiety-inducing activities.

Protection is one such positive player. Let us consider that one aspect of Protection is protecting you from anxiety so much so that you stay clear of relationships, career moves, strenuous sporting activities such as skiing, or even parachute jumping for charity, and so forth – experiences that you may have longed for a taste of. So what might be stopping you? Perhaps an overly protective sense of Protection. With a sense of responsibility for your welfare and wellbeing, Protection is protecting you from getting hurt, protecting you from pain, and from disappointment. In these kinds of instances, however, Protection may well be stopping you from making changes or taking risks which will progress your life along your chosen path. It would be foolhardy to eliminate Protection completely. When you have a player such as this on your team, coach them in ways that offer practical and responsible protection, in ways that do not intrude on your exploring and celebrating life.

Overview of the Detox Formula

To apply the Detox Formula, you will be following these steps:

Tuning in.

    1   Settle down quietly.

    2   Close your eyes and go within.

Tackling the rogue player.

    3   From within, ask for the reason for the problem.

    4   Receive the answer. (If no answer use the Dictionary technique referred to later in this chapter.)

    5   Ask what needs to happen.

    6   Receive the answer.

    7   Coach a potentially healthy rogue to play full-out to support you, or round your rogue player up as a shape.

    8   Negotiate a new role for the rogue player, or release or destroy it!

Embracing the good players.

    9   Invite a supportive player forward.

   10   Ask for suggestions for change.

   11   Embed those suggestions.

   12   Thank your inner mind.

The Detox Formula

1 Settle Down Quietly

Have you switched off your mobile phone, disconnected any other tele-phones or engaged the answering machine? Now you are ready to begin … Arrange yourself comfortably on a chair. Spend a few moments tuning in to the ebb and flow of your breath. Feel the weight of your body on the chair.

2 Close Your Eyes and Go Within

Dive into the inner sense of light within and around you. (The White Light script is included in Chapter 4. An alternative, the Peaceful Place relaxation, is available in Chapter 10.) Readers who have a copy of the audio cassette tape prepared in conjunction with the book may listen to side two to guide them into a state of contemplation.

3 From Within, Ask for the Reason for the Problem

In this state of calm and contemplation, ask the question appertaining to your proposed change.

'Inner mind, what is the reason for <your name>'s smoking?' or

'Inner mind, what is the reason for <your name>'s continuing to smoke?'

'What is the reason for <your name>'s lacking confidence?'

4 Receive the Answer

Listen to the word or words that pop into mind. These represent your rogue players. They may surface one at a time. This is the reason why several sessions may be necessary. Slowly you may open your eyes. Write down the name of the rogue(s). As you become increasingly adept you may find it easy to write words down whilst continuing to keep your eyes closed. For now, slip back into relaxation with your eyes closed.

5 Ask What Needs to Happen

Next ask,

'Inner mind, what needs to happen for <your name> to stop smoking?'
'Inner mind, what needs to happen for <your name> to have confidence?'

6 Receive the Answer

Listen again to the word or words that pop into mind. These represent your positive player(s). Again, only one may come forward. Now slowly open your eyes. Write down the name or names of the positive players.

Remember, as each rogue is eliminated, a substitute player is waiting in the wings to support your chosen team. You will be inviting each supportive substitute forward once the toxic player has been detoxed, once it is out of sight and out of mind.

When rogues and substitutes come forward in equal numbers you may, if you wish, pair a player for elimination with a substitute player – one that will replace it following elimination, and one that is of a positive and healthy persuasion. Alternatively, you may opt for spontaneity and intuition to guide you and welcome whatever positive substitute player pops into mind. When there is more than one rogue, prioritize the rogues that you are going to deal with, and go for the most urgent rogues first.

Sense your inner mind bringing forward the first team member responsible for the problem or issue, and then afterwards sense the next one on your hit-list and so forth. Sense the team member stepping forward.

7 Coach a Potentially Healthy Rogue to Play Full-out to Support You, or Round Your Rogue Player Up as a Shape

You are now ready to begin to imagine your inner mind gathering the sense of the rogue together in some form or other, be it a shape, an object or a box.

Remember, *sensing* is every bit as effective as seeing. Some people who do the detox may not be as visual as others. Search throughout your inner mind for each and every sensation and feeling, each and every phrase or word you have associated with the rogue player. Intention is what matters. Bring forward each and every trace of the rogue, in the form of a shape. Respectfully. Kindly. Lovingly. Bring forward the rogue in its entirety in the form of your chosen shape, and note inwardly what shape you've chosen. Sense the shape, object or box. Be curious to notice what the shape, object or box is made of.

8 Negotiate a New Role for the Rogue Player, or Release or Destroy it!

Next, do whatever it takes to neutralize the shape completely and absolutely. You may choose to destroy the rogue utterly. Alternatively, you may release the shape to a place far, far away, out of sight, out of mind. Acknowledge to yourself when the task is done. You may, for instance, say 'Done'. Sense in yourself when no trace remains, no trace of the shape, or object or box. No trace whatsoever.

When a player is indulging in the behaviour you wish to change, but is nevertheless a positive all-rounder, then proceed by asking the player to come forward with suggestions that will enable you to possess the positive assistance without resorting to the behaviour you have chosen to eliminate.

9 Invite a Supportive Player Forward

Say to yourself: 'On a count of three, <team member's name> come forward! One two three!' Ask, 'Will you agree to support <your name>?' Listen for the 'Yes' or 'No' answer. If a 'No' speaks from within, then ask, 'What is the reason for this?' Listen for, or sense the answer.

The response indicates one of the following:

- That another rogue player has to go first, before the supportive player can be brought into play. (*Sampler 2, page 125, provides a case illustration of the flow of dialogue.*)

- A block is in the way, be it an object or an emotion. (*Sampler 4, page 129, provides a case illustration of the flow of dialogue.*)

- Another supportive team member has to be in place and in play first. (*Sampler 4, page 129, provides a case illustration of the flow of dialogue.*)

In response:

- Ask what needs to happen to persuade the block to go.
- Coach a potentially healthy rogue to play full-out to support you, or round your rogue player up as a shape. Reread Chapter 10 for more information about rounding-up rogues.
- Invite the relevant supportive player to come forward.

If you receive a 'No' response from a player who is potentially supportive but currently obstructive, then you may need to invite it to step forward in a different capacity. Invite it to step forward in order to support you. You will, of course, then need to coach it in the manner described above.

10 Ask for Suggestions for Change

When the initial answer is 'Yes', however, then say within, 'Please come forward with your suggestions.' Then listen.

11 Embed those Suggestions

Say within, 'Inner mind, embed those ideas/suggestions/beliefs/wise words and report when you've done.' You may register the success of the planting by saying 'Done', once you sense the new ideas have been embedded within. Welcome the new positive player(s) to your team.

12 Thank Your Inner Mind

Now spend some moments thanking your inner mind, pointing out all of the positive and advantageous benefits you have gained and will continue to gain as this work goes ahead properly, correctly and permanently. Finally, allow yourself to open your eyes gently and slowly.

Wiggle your fingers and toes, and bring yourself back into the room. The seeds of a new you are planted within the core of your inner being. Write down the suggestions that arose if you wish to do so.

Each day, whenever you choose to spend time in mind detoxing, you can potentially change your opinion of yourself and increasingly become more positive.

Detox Dialogue Samplers

After learning about the Detox Formula this far, spend some time in the mind of Rosa, Simon, Hazel and Roberta, observing their experience of the detox process. They will demonstrate the flow of dialogue exchange in the process. Each detox develops the dialogue to show you how to navigate and negotiate your way through, when blocks appear, and when players present challenges. Do bear in mind that the team members included here are for illustrative purposes only, and that the team members who come forward under your captaincy will reflect your own unique choices. By reading these samplers, you will feel at ease with the formula and have a clearer idea of what is going to happen in the process of coaching your inner team.

Each of the samplers, and the follow-ups, begins from within a state of contemplation, and therefore start at step 3 of the detox formula.

Sampler 1: A Detox to Deal with Stress

3   From within, ask for the reason for the problem.

Rosa: Mind, what is the reason for Rosa's feeling stressed?

4   Receive the answer.

Mind: Heaviness.

5   Ask what needs to happen to begin to change.

Rosa: What needs to happen for Rosa to feel lighter?

6   Receive the answer.

Mind: Confidence.

7   ... round your rogue player up as a shape.

(Inner mind brings forward team player Heaviness in the shape of a wooden square draped with a black cloak.)

8   ... destroy it!

(Mind reports setting fire to the square draped with the black cloak. A gentle breeze carries the residual ash and dust far, far away.)

Mind:	Done!

9   Invite a supportive player forward.

Rosa:	On a count of three, Confidence come forward. One, two, three. Do you agree to support Rosa?
Confidence:	Yes.

10   Ask for suggestions for change.

Rosa:	Please come forward with your suggestions.
Confidence:	Be lighter and happier. Take more care of your health. Take more time to relax.

11   Embed those suggestions.

Rosa:	Inner mind, embed those suggestions and report when you've done.
Mind:	Done.
Rosa:	Welcome to the team, Confidence.

12   Thank your inner mind . . .

Sampler 2: A Detox to Build Belief, and Reinforcement of the Belief

3   From within, ask for the reason for the problem.

Simon:	Mind, what is the reason for Simon not feeling intelligent?

4   Receive the answer.

Mind: Negative.

5   Ask what needs to happen.

Simon: What needs to happen for Simon to begin to
                 realize how much intelligence he has?

6   Receive the answer.

Mind: Believe in himself.

7   . . . round your rogue player up as a shape.

(Inner mind brings forward team player Negative in the shape of a rotting
peach.)

8   . . . destroy it!

(Inner mind reports wrapping the peach in old newspaper. The wrapped
fruit is then put into the rubbish bin. The dustbin collectors take the
wrapped fruit away. The Rubbish Collectors are discussed in Chapter 11.)

Mind: Done!

9   Invite a supportive player forward.

Simon: On a count of three, Belief come forward. One,
                 two, three. Will you agree to support Simon?

Belief: Yes.

10   Ask for suggestions for change.

Simon: Please come forward with your suggestions.

Belief: Everything is in the mind.
                 Nothing can stop you but yourself.
                 You can overcome any obstacle.

11   Embed those suggestions.

Simon: Inner mind, embed those beliefs and report
                 when you've done.

Mind: Done!

You may if you wish invite the quality opposite to the original problem to come forward for reinforcement.

9   Invite a supportive player forward.

Simon: On a count of three, Intelligence come forward. One, two, three. Intelligence, will you agree to support Simon?

Intelligence: Yes.

10   Ask for suggestions for change.

Simon: Please come forward with your suggestions.

Intelligence: I'm intelligent.
I'm competent.
I have no fears.

11   Embed those suggestions.

Simon: Inner mind, embed those suggestions and report when you've done.

Mind: Done!

Simon: Welcome to the team, Belief and Intelligence.

12   Thank your inner mind …

Sampler 3: A Detox to Build Confidence

Follow the process of how to coach a potentially healthy rogue to play full-out, and reinforce by inviting the player at the centre of your session forward to conclude the detox.

3   From within, ask for the reason for the problem.

Hazel: Mind, what is the reason for Hazel's lack of self-confidence?

4   Receive the answer.

Mind: She feels different – alone.

5   Ask what needs to happen.

Hazel: What needs to happen for Hazel to feel different and confident?

6   Receive the answer.

Mind: Gratitude.

7   Coach a potentially healthy rogue to play full-out to support you.

Hazel: Alone, will you agree to be different and have confidence?

Alone: Yes.

8   Negotiate a new role for the rogue player.

Hazel: Please come forward with your suggestions.

Alone: Be yourself.
              Do not seek approval.
              Follow that which you believe in and feel is right.

Hazel: Mind, embed those suggestions and report when you've done.

Mind: Done!

9   Invite a supportive player forward.

Hazel: On a count of three, Gratitude come forward. One, two, three. Will you agree to support Hazel?

Gratitude: Yes.

10   Ask for suggestions for change.

Hazel: Please come forward with your suggestions.

Gratitude: Be more positive.
              Be more content.
              See the good in everything.

11   Embed those suggestions.

Hazel: Inner mind, embed those suggestions and report
                when you've done.

Mind: Done!

9   Reinforce by deferring to the reason for the session.

Invite a supportive player to come forward.

Hazel: On a count of three, Confidence come forward.
                One, two, three. Will you agree to support
                Hazel?

Confidence: Yes.

10   Ask for suggestions for change.

Hazel: Please come forward with your suggestions.

Confidence: Believe in yourself more.
                Communicate more effectively.
                Free yourself from fear.

11   Embed those suggestions.

Hazel: Inner mind, embed those suggestions and report
                when you've done.

Mind: Done!

Hazel: Welcome to the team Alone, Gratitude and
                Confidence.

12 Thank your Inner mind ...

Sampler 4: A Detox to Deal with Embarrassment

This coaching session involved the revisiting of a team player who initially refused to support. This sampler also includes a follow-up detox.

3   From within, ask for the reason for the problem.

Roberta: Mind, what is the reason for Roberta's feeling
            embarrassed?

4   Receive the answer.

Mind: Anxiety.

5   Ask what needs to happen.

Roberta: What needs to happen for Roberta to begin to let
            go of anxiety?

6   Receive the answer.

Mind: Positive.

7   … round your rogue player up as a shape.

(Inner mind brings forward Anxiety in the shape of a triangle made of
aluminium.)

8   … destroy it!

(Inner mind places the triangle shape made of aluminium in a furnace
and melts it down, leaving no trace.)

Mind: Done!

9   Invite a supportive player forward.

Roberta: On a count of three, Positive come forward. One,
            two, three. Will you agree to support Roberta?

Positive: No.

Roberta: What is the reason for this?

Positive: There is a knot of wood blocking the way that
            has been resident for a long time and doesn't
            want to go.

5   Ask what needs to happen.

Roberta: What needs to happen to persuade the knot of
            wood to go?

6   Receive the answer.

Positive: She needs to believe she is good.

9   Reinvite a supportive player forward.

Roberta: On a count of three, Belief come forward. One,
                two, three. Will you agree to support Roberta?

Belief: Yes.

10   Ask for suggestions for change.

Roberta: Please come forward with your suggestions.

Belief: I believe in her honesty.
                I believe in her success.
                I believe in her being good in the company of
                others.

11   Embed those suggestions.

Roberta: Inner mind, embed those beliefs and report
                when you've done.

Mind: Done!

9   Invite a supportive player forward.

Roberta: On a count of three, Positive come forward. One,
                two, three. Will you agree to support Roberta?

Positive: Yes.

10   Ask for suggestions for change.

Roberta: Please come forward with your suggestions.

Positive: Be practical.
                Be steady.
                Be realistic.

11   Embed those suggestions.

Roberta: Inner mind, embed those suggestions and report
                when you've done.

Mind:	Done!
Roberta:	Welcome to the team, Belief and Positive.

12   Thank your inner mind ...

Roberta's follow-up detox:

3   From within, ask for the reason for the problem.

Roberta: Inner mind, what is the reason for Roberta's feeling there's something wrong?

4   Receive the answer.

Inner mind: Nervous.

5   Ask what needs to happen.

Roberta: What needs to happen for Roberta to begin to feel less nervous?

6   Receive the answer.

Inner mind: Confidence.

7   ... round your rogue player up as a shape.

(Inner mind brings forward Nervous in the shape of a root ball.)

8   ... release it!

(Inner mind chooses to release, rather than to destroy, reporting that the root ball has been there a long time. Inner mind finds a very special forest, far, far away, one where the root ball can be transplanted. In a further follow-up the root ball may be destroyed. For now, respect the decision as presented by inner mind.)

Mind: Done!

9   Invite a supportive player forward.

Roberta: On a count of three, Confidence come forward. One, two, three. Will you agree to support Roberta?

Confidence: No.

Roberta: What is the reason for this?

Confidence: Shy.

7   . . . round your rogue player up as a shape.

(Inner mind brings forward Shy in the shape of a rectangular block of wood.)

8   . . . destroy it!

(Inner mind reports having hurled the rectangular block of wood into the sea. It is out of sight in the midst of the waves. Over time it has rotted to dust and disappeared.)

Mind: Gone!

9   Reinvite a supportive player forward.

Roberta: On a count of three, Confidence come forward.
One, two, three. Will you agree to support
Roberta?

Confidence: Yes.

10   Ask for suggestions for change.

Roberta: Please come forward with your suggestions.

Confidence: Be more relaxed in company.
Be open and honest.
Focus and enjoy the moment.

11   Embed those suggestions.

Roberta: Inner mind, embed those beliefs and report
when you've done.

Mind: Done!

Roberta: Welcome to the team, Confidence.

12   Thank your inner mind …

These sampler scripts have given you an experience of how you can expect the dialogue to flow and grow during a personal detox session or follow-up.

You may choose to develop your own script(s) based upon these recommendations. You may even create a template, leaving blank spaces to introduce the suggestions for change as you intuit them. Do allow for each of the possible outcomes in constructing this kind of template – for example a block, or a potentially supportive player holding back initially whilst a fellow team member is eliminated. You may also choose, as Peter did in Chapter 4, to digress in such a way that complements your own personal style and preferred vocabulary. In other words, as you become increasingly assured, you are encouraged to go with the flow and to coach in a way that offers clarity and understanding for you.

A later script, Sampler 5, will guide you through offering a choice to a rogue team player (*see page 139*).

Signed, Sealed and Delivered

By following this step-by-step detox formula you have taken time to go within and engage in a dialogue with your inner mind. The conversation has taken place in that part of you where all learning and all change takes place – the changing room within.

When you gain rapport with your inner mind you effectively allow room for change – room to give birth to fresh ideas, to scatter their seeds, and for them to embed. Follow-up sessions will water and nourish the seeds, allowing growth and inner acknowledgement, as you sense the subtle change of your innermost thoughts.

You will be surprised to discover you have introduced new thoughts into your life which, without a Mind Detox, may never have entered into your head! You will be even more surprised to discover that, one day soon, you will realize you are being that which you wish to become!

Troubleshooting

What to Do When No Reason Comes Forward

When no reason for a particular behaviour, feeling or response comes forward, you may resort to one of the two options that follow:

- The Dictionary Technique.
- Refer to the original problem.

Both of these are designed to provide a safe space in which the inner mind can yield up the fruits of its boundless creativity, its capacity to generate images, ideas, words and thoughts. The reason for this round-about route is that the inner mind often shies away from openly presenting what it harbours: it needs a prepared format into which it can insert what it has dreamt up.

The Dictionary Technique

On some occasions, having put a question to the inner mind, the response may be one of silence: an apparent 'Don't Know'. One technique you may introduce is The Dictionary. Bring forward into your inner mind a picture, or some other notion, of a huge, leather-bound dictionary – with its title inlaid in gold-leaf writing on the spine and the front cover. Begin to be aware of the pages beginning to stir, as you respectfully open the cover and thumb through the pages. Let the pages flutter backwards and forwards – from A to Z and back to A. Eventually the pages come to rest. You are curious to notice the pages come to rest at a particular letter of the alphabet. Notice the letter of the alphabet at the top of the page. Having done so, let your gaze travel down the page, noting the words beginning with that particular letter. You may be even more curious to notice one word, bolder and larger than all of the others, pop out from the page. Note this word. Take this word as one representing the team member you wish to speak to. Begin by asking whether it is appropriate to speak to that team member.

When to Defer to the Reason for the Session

Alternatively, when no reason steps forward, you may simply defer to any word that sums up your reason for embarking on the particular session. So, say that you have set aside time to deal with Stress, simply invite Stress to come forward and ask her the question directly.

As you may have noted in Sampler 3, you may also choose to bring forward the team player representing the reason for the coaching session when building qualities that you view yourself lacking. These may include confidence, intelligence, courage, discipline, focus and so on. Having heard the suggestions voiced by other supporting players, invite Confidence forward to have the final word.

Appointment with Fear

How do you deal with negative members, such as Fear, who might choose to stay? Fear, Scared, or Fear under another name, may have figured already in some of the coaching you've done this far. Coaching to free yourself of anxiety and panic may well involve you in a dialogue with Fear. For this reason, the instruction that follows is included to give you some additional options to handle the coaching of Fear. These options may expand your experience, and provide you with some additional negotiating skills to play with. Fear is a player that seeks out a position on the inner team time and time again. Fear will seek out and find a way of attack, when an aspect of your life is changing, or when you've decided to take on something new.

 In Georgina's case she simply wished to relax more and take life less seriously. Fear was strongly opposed to these changes. She strode out as a large, fat sheet of metal, pushing against Georgina, physically resisting change by virtue of her sheer weight and bulk. The team player offered further justification for her actions by adding that her presence acted as a barrier, offering a sheet of protection around Georgina's heart. 'I don't like change!' she barked, and was seemingly determined to stay put.

Fear is often present when you decide, having listened to your heart, to follow your heart's desire. Fear is often felt as an undercurrent of anxiety filling your stomach, colouring your thoughts with shades of grey to black and weighing them down with Worry. Fear blocks you up and locks you up.

The lock is turned to tighten your stomach muscles into knots, and to elicit feelings and states of mind that are far from supportive, that do not empower you to move forward successfully towards and through life's journey.

Let us say you are experiencing feelings of Fear in the form of one of Fear's family members, such as Anxiety, before some event in your life. You may ask inner mind the question, 'Inner mind what is the reason for <your name>'s feeling <family member's name e.g. Anxiety>?' In response, the F-word itself, 'Fear', may come forward.

Having identified Fear, you can present the team member with a choice. Up to this point in the detox process, the unsatisfactory team members have not been offered a choice. They have all been ordered off the field. As you progress with doing detox dialogues you may, if you wish, choose always to give unsatisfactory and rogue team players a choice.

The choice:

- ask the member whether it wishes to channel the energy of Fear creatively, in some way that can support you positively and advantageously throughout the presenting situation; or

- ask Fear if it prefers to step down from the team and be released or eliminated from your inner mind.

Wait a moment, and listen to the choice that Fear makes. Suppose that Fear agrees to support you by channelling the feeling of fear in a way that sustains and empowers you creatively throughout the situation. You can then proceed by asking the reformed player to come forward with three suggestions that will be effective in promoting the desired change. Ask Fear to embed those suggestions in your inner mind.

When Fear decides to be dropped from the team altogether, gather this rogue player together into some form in the usual way. A note of TLC (tender, loving care) is needed here. Fear is a frightened player and is to be treated with gentleness. Put on your kid gloves. Search throughout your inner mind for each and every sensation and feeling of Fear. As you have already experienced, intention is what matters. Bring forward each and every trace of Fear, in the form of a shape. Respectfully. Kindly. Lovingly. As you are accustomed, note inwardly what shape you have chosen and be curious, too, to notice what the shape is made of. Proceed with the release or the elimination.

So, let me reiterate that last point. If you can't beat them, allow them to join – but on your terms! Negative team members may stay on board, but only with the following proviso: in each and every case, they must agree to channel what was their negative energy creatively and positively in ways that will contribute to your wellbeing and success.

 Trudy desired to be more self-disciplined with respect to her personal training. Fear stepped forward as the prime reason for her experience of lack of discipline. Fear opted without reservation to help put her back on a disciplined track. Fear chose to rechannel her intention with:

- Determination
- Preparation
- Organization.

One choice the rogue cannot be allowed to make is to stay, and not support. You may remind robust and rebellious rogue members of the choice available to them now that you have resolved to change your life.

You may need to revisit this session until you are successful, but do persevere, and keep going back to it until you get what you want. The detox dialogue will gradually dilute the toxicity of the player and its influence on your behaviour.

Having started to unblock and unlock yourself, you may now wish to invite Fear's opposite number to come forward.

Inviting the Opposite of Fear Forward

Whether Fear opted to focus upon creative support, or to be dropped from the team, you may now choose to invite whatever you consider to be the opposite of the rogue player forward. For example, you may decide to champion Courage or Brave and invite either player forward to share its suggestions with you. Alternatively, you may invite any other positive player forward that can best support your outcome.

You may consider the members Courage and Brave as actually being the member Fear, but having shifted position favourably and thereby having transformed itself. Having moved from Fear towards Courage, one has shifted several places along a continuum in a positive orientation. When you consider yourself as moving towards a quality, a belief, a behaviour, you are immediately empowered.

Another example may be of moving from a state of Conflict within, to a state of Peace. Peace is really the other side of the same coin. With practice, you can develop the capacity to hold both sides of a position in your mind, and move from your past position through a positive shift, from 'I am not …' to 'I am …' For some, it can be tempting to stay with the familiar. As we shift our associations of happiness onto Intelligence, and a Belief in our Intelligence, the team reorganization can begin to lighten our load. Likewise, as we move from a past position of Fear to one of Courage, the more courageous you feel, the stronger you feel, and as your inner Lion takes you on, and leads you in life, the less Fear will have power over you.

Sampler 5: A Detox to Deal with the Fear Underlying Bottled-up Stress

This detox sampler demonstrates how to offer rogues such as Fear and Stress the option of reform. As before, this detox begins from within a state of contemplation, and assumes that you have already passed through steps 1 and 2 of the Detox Formula.

3   From within, ask for the reason for the problem.

Lynne: Mind, what is the reason for Lynne bottling up her stress?

4   Receive the answer.

Mind: Fear.

5   Ask what needs to happen …

Lynne: What needs to happen for Lynne to begin to let go of bottling up her stress?

6   Receive the answer.

Mind: Defend herself from stress.

7   Offer your rogue a choice: either round your rogue player up as a shape, or offer the chance of channelling the negative aspect in positive ways.

Lynne: Fear, you have a choice. You can choose to support Lynne or you can choose to be released and eliminated. What do you choose?

Fear: To support.

8   Negotiate a new role for the rogue player.

Lynne: Fear, please come forward with your suggestions for your new and supporting role.

Fear: To walk in the fresh air.
            To relax in the bath.
            To take lots of exercise.

Lynne: Inner mind, embed those suggestions and report when you've done.

Mind: Done!

9   Invite a supportive player forward.

Lynne: On a count of three, Defend come forward. One,
             two, three. Will you agree to support Lynne?

Defend: Yes.

10   Ask for suggestions for change.

Lynne: Please come forward with your suggestions.

Defend: Be calm.
             Go swimming.
             Fly a kite.

11   Embed those suggestions.

Lynne: Inner mind, embed those suggestions and report
             when you've done.

Mind: Done!

Reinforce by deferring to the reason for the session.

7   Offer your rogue a choice. Either round your rogue player up as a
     shape, or offer the chance of channelling the negative sensation in
     positive ways.

Lynne: Stress, you have a choice. You can choose to
             support Lynne or you can choose to be released
             and eliminated. What do you choose?

Stress: To support.

8   Negotiate a new role for the rogue player, or release …

Lynne: Stress, please come forward with suggestions
             for your new and supporting role.

Stress: Be consistently calm.
             Be methodical.
             Be prepared.

| Lynne: | Inner mind, embed those suggestions and report when you've done. |
| Mind: | Done! |

You may if you wish invite the opposite quality forward for reinforcement.

9   Invite a supportive player forward.

| Lynne: | On a count of three, Brave come forward. One, two, three. Brave, will you agree to support Lynne? |
| Brave: | Yes. |

10   Ask for suggestions for change.

| Lynne: | Please come forward with your suggestions. |
| Brave: | Listen to your feelings as well as your thoughts. Let go of thinking so much. Remember the times you have been very brave. |

11   Embed those suggestions.

Lynne:	Inner mind, embed those suggestions and report when you've done.
Mind:	Done!
Lynne:	Welcome to the team, Brave.

12   Thank your inner mind ...

Reluctant Team Members

Occasionally, it does happen. You politely ask, but no sense of rogue players or positive players comes forward. You may invite a rogue player to come forward, and the response is a firm 'No'. Fear is one such taciturn player. Pain, Anger and Rejection are others. Curiously, the most taciturn are those players that position themselves in our lives game after game, season after season.

You have two options: to leave it for another day, or gently to persist.

You may agree to set up the detox for another occasion. Play fair with yourself. Sometimes your inner mind may not turn up for a coaching session when rainy, run-out and run-down; feelings really do stop play. So you are just not in the mood. Respect and allow for this.

If you choose to persist gently, and I stress the gentleness, you can ask the following: 'What needs to be in place for the reluctant team member <team member's name> to agree to step forward?' Include the name of the team member when you ask the question.

Sense the word or words that pop into mind. These are players to cushion and support inner mind.

Perhaps the response is one of Safety, and the need to feel safe.

Write down the name of the back-up, cushioning player(s). (By now you may find it easier to write down words whilst keeping your eyes closed. Do not worry if they are rather scrawled – you can always make a fair copy later.)

Having recorded the player's name, slip back into relaxation with your eyes closed. Continue by asking Safety to come forward with three suggestions in the normal way.

With Safety's strategy in place, you can revisit the resisting team member to ask again whether the member will now agree to step forward and play a supporting role. If the answer is yes, by all means continue the dialogue.

If not, then let go of the session until another day. End the session by taking a white-light shower to rinse and release residual toxins. As before, visualize a power-shower of white light streaming down and running into the crown of your head, flowing through and around the body. (The White Light power-shower is included in Chapter 4.)

I cannot emphasize enough that this work is not about bullying the inner mind into play. Mind Detox is a process of negotiation and gentle persuasion. It is non-judgmental and should be conducted with kindness and due respect for the inner mind and its vulnerability.

Teams with Proven Success

In this section you are about to meet a selection of inner team members who have collectively contributed to the success of their captains. The weight-loss and stopping-smoking teams, in particular, demonstrate how internal discussions may develop in your inner mind. Do remember that your cast of players may well be different. These five teams are examples only. Also, the issue you wish to work on may be different from the problems included here. This being the case, you can still use the Detox Formula and apply the practice to your special case.

The case studies provide insight as to how, with practice, you can coach your inner team. You can learn to negotiate, to persuade and to lead players towards following new strategies and tactics. You can let go of players that no longer have a role in the team, and bring into your team the aces that have been held in reserve.

For guidance and inspiration, you may choose to read about the single issue that most concerns you. You can check over both the line-up of supportive players, and those listed in the rogues' gallery. Some players you will choose to transfer in, and others you will, more than likely, transfer out.

Transfers

Transferring players in or out is a team-and time-management issue. If you've chosen to begin a Mind Detox for weight loss, and you are presently three stone overweight, then you will require the member Patience to be playing around the clock. After several sessions and a few weeks, the pounds will begin to let go and roll off. As you feel lighter by the fewest of pounds, you will feel empowered by your team's result, and that fresh fuel will power your journey onward to continuing success. As the momentum gathers, Patience may not be such a premium player and you can choose to transfer in Persistence to keep you on track. So players will come and go. When you want a player back on your inner team, you will have learned to ask it to come forward and to invite fresh suggestions.

The player's suggestions a few weeks down the road may well be very different, because you will have stepped so far forward in your journey.

As you engage in the detox process, you will sense each session beginning at a slightly different place along your path. By employing the detox process, you are in many ways evolving, and transforming in subtle ways. It is not appropriate to place a bookmark in the place you left off, because you are in a sense always on the move – as you gain clarity and understanding, and experience a subtle shift in consciousness. A notebook is therefore better than a bookmark, and will let you keep track of inner strengthening and inner growth. Reflecting on your positive experiences will champion further a winning team.

Confidence and Self-esteem Building

How we long to wear the absolute crown! To be the Air of Confidence. This is confidence stepping out at its strongest. It is a sense of inner confidence that is free of reliance upon props and status symbols, such as achievement, success, approval or recognition – a confidence that is a constant presence, whatever life throws into the Air for us to handle. Occasionally withdrawn, we long to break out of our shell, to take up this crown of confidence, and to sit on the throne of personal power, to be in control of, and rule over, ourselves. We long to be in the seat of our true and fullest self-expression.

A lack of confidence, or a belief that one lacks confidence, is a core problem in many people's lives. Most of the time, this is a lack of confidence to express what you really feel. Lack of confidence is often tied in with a lack of self-esteem and a need to seek approval. Moreover, our tendency to punish ourselves by thinking badly of ourselves is another way in which the same problem manifests itself. To esteem ourselves, to feel comfortable and confident with others and within ourselves, is a giant step on the path to freedom and liberation. When we have this, we are on our way to gaining our wings, because so much follows from, and through, this solid sense of being strong, right in the very heart of our being.

With Confidence and Self-respect enrolled in your inner teams, your potential for healing is boundless. The first step is to put yourself in the picture, to put yourself centre-stage in your life. Once centred in yourself – once self-centred – you can take time to listen to the communications inside yourself, which so often speak volumes. These communications have often been compiled to form a book of interior wisdom. A book of experience. This inner book of wisdom and experience, bound not in leather but by your feelings about them, is kept in the basement of your inner mind. Some inner books of wisdom lay unopened, and unrecognized forever. Some are touched, the first pages turned, then discarded because their journey is long and winding, and may stir further your unease. Others are picked up. They are held, and they are hugged, by Acceptance, and by Love and then left to Let Go, in order that their owners can move forward with Freedom, with Liberation and with Wings, and begin to polish the jewels of wisdom that are written in the book. Some are sat upon for years, and years, and years, asking repeatedly to be listened to, asking to be dusted down, asking for a hearing. Asking for a reading – with and through our Adult, and grown-up, eyes. Sometimes it seems that the very people who brought us up have brought us down – so it seems. During a 're-reading' we can discover how as a child we misread, misinterpreted, misheard, or took so literally the oft-repeated words and communications spoken from on high. Our parents once seemed next to God – so our experience and our belief told us. Now, as grown-ups, perhaps with children of our own, we have an opportunity to dry the tears of our still sometimes inconsolable Inner Child and to begin to re-read this book with a view to gaining clarity and understanding, acknowledging, forgiving and letting go. We can say to our Inner Child: 'I promise, this will never happen to you again. I love you and will always protect you.' Remembered, and recovered, and brought back into play, your Inner Child is the team member who can help you to keep your eye on the ball, can keep you energized, maintain your excitement in simple pleasures and keep your body and mind feeling and looking younger for longer. Of all your team members, this is the one who knows the most about play, and creative play. She will keep you amused for hours and keep boredom at bay.

Gratitude may open your eyes to what you have learned through your experiences and so enable you to move on with your kit-bag of experiences and Smile, Smile, Smile!

Relationships heal. Relationships that acknowledge the best and the brightest in us help us to heal. These are relationships with partners and friends to whom we are guided – people that we say we 'recognized' as being our teachers in some way – people with whom we experience ourselves, and our potential for greatness. Sometimes relationships appear to do the opposite. Relationships into which we are drawn and to which we are attracted so often appear gilded and glossy and golden but, after an elapse of time, end up providing more bitter experiences to goad us and to gloat over us. Through them we choose to gather more evidence to confirm our sense of lack, of what we believe we are not! Nevertheless, the significance of even these relationships is also for us to experience ourselves, and to gain an awareness of our potential for inner power and greatness. Eventually they can and do bring us that truth. Eventually one of these relationships may cause us abruptly to interrupt the internal mind-field of thought.

When such a time comes, the mind and the heart explode. Fragments of ash and dust settle down beside us as we sit on our sofa drifting through the fog of our emotions. We sit on a sofa at sea with the dregs of Confidence draining out of us as Depression enjoys an endless round of cups of coffee and TV soap operas. We are fully armed with Self-pity and Self-loathing. Depression sends out to its friends an open invitation: join us at the wake! Rejection, Abandonment, Insignificance, Smallness, Cynicism, Insecurity, Fear and Failure come around and throw a few more toxins into the pot. They match each other, pound for pound, pint for pint.

The Poor Me team sit before their inner Judge and Jury to savour the despondency. Poor Me has 'Victim' tattooed right through, like a stick of Brighton rock.

Wisdom and Experience may join us on the sofa and speak – with trepidation. Wisdom and Experience are very familiar with being shouted down. One word at a time. One sentence at a time. They stroke our heart and lead us to some sense of understanding. Muddled perhaps:

'Enough is enough!'

'You do not have to do this to yourself.'

'There is another way.'

'Life can be different.'

'You are worth more.'

'You can change.'

'Sleep on it. You'll feel better in the morning.'

'Tomorrow is another day!'

The angel is at your shoulder, beside you on the sofa of desolation, radiating in all of the fulsome magnificence that you cannot see, feel or hear. It is as though she has access to all of the unpolished jewels, and she passes them as whispers before our tearful eyes. It is as though she holds the keys.

Even then her inner promises can fall on deaf ears. Rarely are we deaf indefinitely. The light of our inner understanding eventually flickers on. Suddenly, and seemingly out of the blue, a very small thing, like a word in the wrong place at the wrong time, and sometimes in the right place at the right time, brings on Break-down, and game stops play – so completely, so absolutely.

'Why Me? Why This? Why Now?', asked Robin Norwood in her book of the same name. Of course there are many reasons. So often, though, a lack of the team members Love, Respect, and Esteem for ourselves are major players at these times. In their place have muscled in the rogues Loathing, Guilty, Wrong and Fear. These players bait, berate and beat us Blue with feeling, and keep us Bad. They keep us in a corner and, as we outgrow one corner, they can, in more severe cases, find another bigger one to push into and hold us bound. Corner. Rut. Trough. Pit. Den. It was by God's Grace, Daniel escaped the lion's den. Possibly by that same grace, and by our beginning to take on Captaincy of our inner mind-fields, can we begin to escape our life-disabling dens.

As you turn the cover of your own book of wisdom, you may well note whether the title sheet is stamped: Long Overdue.

Some of the Confidence Boosters

Acceptance
- I easily accept mistakes, letting go quickly.
- I am love and I love myself.
- I am value and I value myself.
- I am strength and I grow stronger.

Belief
- I increasingly believe in my strength of will.
- I nurture and care for myself.
- I believe in my own ability.
- My confidence and self-respect are an inspiration to others.
- Others sense my positive vibration.
- I believe my photograph expresses my special qualities.
- I trust my voice recording on my answering machine.

Booster
- I remind you to keep loving every part of yourself.
- I help you to be confident in the present moment.
- I offer positive words of encouragement.

Comfortable
- I feel comfortable with others and within myself.
- I feel natural with myself and with others.

Confidence
- I remind you of how interesting you are.
- I encourage you to make your own judgements.
- I help you move towards peace of mind.

- I help you move towards serenity.
- I am confident, and my confidence is constant.
- I am courageous.

Creativity
- I am assertive through kindness.
- I am confident in my decisions.
- I do not give in from a position of weakness.

Ego
- I have confidence.
- I have respect for myself.
- I have happiness.
- I have pride.

Positivity
- I break through the circle of negativity.

Qualities
- I am caring.
- I am loving.
- I accept.

Validation
- I help you to like yourself.
- I help you to let go of rationalizing everything you do.
- I help keep you focused.

Strength
- I do not give in when I sense I will deny my sense of self by doing so.
- I am free of the need to be approved of.
- I take action from a position of inner power.

Success
- I help you remain emotionally centred.

Will Power
- I can.
- I will.
- I want to.
- I believe.

- I shut out the negative.
- I acclaim the positive.
- I reinforce the outcome.

Some of the Tricksters

Afraid	Intimidation
Anger	Limiting
Approval	Negative
Attention	Self-conscious
Awkward	Self-control
Bad	Self-doubt
Belief	Sensitive
Block	Shy
Critical	Small
Defect	Unconfident
Disrespect	Uneasy
Embarrassed	Unworthy
Fear	Weak
Guilty	Withdrawn
Humiliation	Worthless
Insecurity	Wrong
Insignificant	

Weight Loss

When clients arrive with a view to losing weight, like you they always know everything there is to know about nutrition and diet. When diets do not work, it is often because you have been programmed to eat for another reason, and it may have nothing to do with normal eating satisfaction. Sometimes you are carrying emotional weight that is blocking the release of the physical weight. Sometimes, when a person lets go of the emotional weight, the physical will begin to shift.

Anger, Sadness, Pain, Control, unhappy Memories. Get the suitcase down from on top of the wardrobe. Dust off the cobwebs. Pack the weight into the suitcase and blow it up!

To change eating patterns you can, over time, work to access those members of your inner team that appear to be making it seemingly impossible for you to lose weight and keep the weight off.

You need to get in touch with the team members that diets cannot possibly reach. What you need to do is detox to discover when you first started eating for a reason, other than to nourish your body. Any kind of eating that overrides that satisfied feeling is for extra satisfaction. It is this extra satisfaction that needs dealing with.

You may find that in a few sessions you begin to change the eating behaviour that no longer serves you, freeing you to be a more positive and productive person.

What follows is a dialogue with those members of one client's inner team that had worked against her losing weight. It is intended to give you some insight as to how, by gaining agreement with your inner team members, you can work to help change your behaviour.

A weighty team of players hung in the wardrobe of Carrie's inner mind. They went by the names of Comfort, Limiting, Fear, Uncertainty, Lazy, Persistence, and a coat called Patience. All hung alongside the size 10 black dress that had once fitted. Carrie remembered days … and nights … wearing the dress … enjoying a sense of elegance and stature. She had long forgotten what kicked in to frame the shape of the body now.

The black dress has hung through 20 summers, waiting for the day to come when she decided to remember what she had forgotten, and so … let go of the weight on her mind, and allow the weight on her body to let go and move forward towards the size she remembers she once was, and the shape she wants her future to be.

Comfort is the first to come forward. Comfort wants to comfort with carbohydrates – macaroni cheese, pizzas and cartons of creamy custard. Mother Comfort offers treats – oodles of her favourite Chinese cuisine to coax the reclusive and the reluctant forward to perform unsavoury tasks. Instant rewards. Instant gratification. Instant comfort. Limiting her bulging body and her buoyant creative mind. Comfort and Limiting have a close working relationship.

Limiting lowers her expectations. Limiting lowers her standards. Limiting minimizes what Carrie can expect for herself in all other aspects of her life. Limiting limits the amount of 'real nourishment' she gains from food, by limiting the range of available choices. Limiting happily allows Comfort to molly-coddle with large quantities of mushy macaroni, because Comfort paves the path for Limiting to continue to narrow the range of available choices.

With such low levels of expectation, the future is sown with seeds that feed Fear. Fear moves life forward and ploughs the fields of the conscious mind with thoughts that scatter, thoughts that distract ... and thoughts that keep the conscious house in order. Thoughts that keep Carrie from exploring creative territory. It is as though the blinds are drawn – shutting out the voice of creativity. Fear keeps the woman distracted by pursuits other than those that honour the person Carrie would like to be. The woman who is the writer. The woman in the black dress who stood on the balcony some 20 years ago and thought she knew the shape of things to come. Fear finds her so easily distracted. It's a great game! Each time she moves to open the blinds, to sit down ... to be still ... and write, Fear presents something to be done, an urgent and so unnecessary task. Fear has always moved her life forward ... in ways she wants to go. Fear goes with the flow ... Every fleeting moment focused on the possibility of 'fame' is squashed by Fear and Uncertainty. It is too painful to be still, to sit by still waters and, after all, she is too Lazy to get started.

Lazy. Too Lazy to buy all the ingredients to make her life better. Too Lazy to mix and combine all the best of life into a recipe that creates her success. Too Lazy to cook up anything creative. Too Lazy to cook. Lazy is lying in a lair.

Persistence panics. You're not Lazy. How can you be Lazy, when you're so Persistent? You've Persisted at getting the results that you're getting. You've Persisted at putting on so much weight. You have persisted at learning to eat under all circumstances except hunger. Lazy is lying. Now you need to learn more Patience. Patience to care. Patience to choose healthy ingredients. Patience to combine all the best of life into a recipe that creates success. Patience to cook up creative writings. Patience to cook.

Patience stepped forward. Reluctantly Patience came forward in a vision of a coat. Patience tried the coat for size. The coat was made of rough matted hair. The coat itched and created an aggravating sense of discomfort.

Resistance stepped forward. 'I don't like the coat. It is like one my Mother would wear.' Patience remodels the coat, changing it to a style and shape Resistance liked. The coat resembles a pink comforting mohair blanket.

Patience wraps it around her.

Lack of Patience has contributed to Carrie's eating fast and furiously. Lack of Patience has caused pain in both body and mind. Lack of Patience has found comfort in eating to satisfy needs other than normal nourishment.

As you may well have experienced, eating for comfort is like being addicted to a drug. You are on a short high, having satisfied your craving. Habitually eating carbohydrate for comfort leads to a vicious circle, where you get hooked. This habit seeks out people who are needy of attention and of love and of comfort … rather than sitting down and writing, or exercising, you swallow some food. It is a temporary fix only, because afterwards there are no articles, no short stories, no novellas, no action. You've not written anything new and interesting and you are still hungry for comfort. So when the fix wears off, the urge to be comforted returns … another fix … more food … more fat … more weight.

An umpire stepped forward named Stop.

'Just stop!' she cried. 'Put an end to this sabotage ... claim back your life ... if you get the urge to eat, drink a glass of water, or a cup of herbal tea ... go out for a walk and comfort yourself with the visual things ... with beauty ... with the scent of flowers ... instead of the smell and taste of stodge.'

'Patience, do you agree to have a bigger part in the woman's life?'

Patience reluctantly replies, 'I'll try.' This time I persist. 'Patience, in order for the woman to move forward in her life and to let go of the weight of the past, and the weight on her body, you need to allow Patience to be an important part in her life.' 'I'll follow her round in the pink coat and put out a saucer of milk to remind her to be more patient every day.'

Successful Weightlifters

These are the team members to coach to maintain a frame of mind concentrated and focused on arriving at the weight you wish to be.

Belief
- I believe I can maintain my weight and not go back to eating as before.
- I believe I will look really good.
- I believe I will be healthier.
- I control my body and mind.

Body Image
- I move towards love for my body.
- I move towards gratefulness for my body.
- I move towards liking my body.

Comfort
- I find other ways to feel comfortable
- I find other relaxing ways.
- I allow more time to prepare my appearance rather than getting ready in a rush.
- I spend more time doing other things, or just doing nothing.

Confidence	■ I let go of judging myself.
	■ I accept myself.
	■ I accept mistakes are only human.
Control	■ Happiness grows as I gain control.
	■ I'm moving forward.
	■ I'm on my way.
	■ I am increasingly in control of why I eat and when I eat.
Creativity	■ I find other things to fill the time.
	■ I watch and participate in a video-based exercise programme.
	■ I drink water instead of alcohol.
Enjoyment	■ I enjoy retaining some energy for myself.
Euphoria	■ I feel euphoria wearing clothes which once did not fit.
	■ Feeling fitter gives me a buzz.
Exercise	■ I exercise every day.
Fruit/ Vegetable	■ I feel positive eating fruit and vegetables.
	■ The more I eat the more positive I feel.
	■ Fruit and vegetables fight fat.
Focus	■ I keep focused on friendship.
	■ I keep focused on goals.
	■ I keep focused on achievements.
	■ I keep focused on the clothes I will buy.
	■ I focus and prepare an idea of my order before I go into a restaurant.
	■ I remain balanced.

Healthy
- I think about what I put in my mouth.
- It is part of my lifestyle to put food into my mouth that will make me feel happy 10 minutes later.
- I eat food which is worth eating, food which is valuable.
- I love eating vegetables.
- I avoid fast food.
- I choose wisely.
- Sugar is out.

Heart
- I love.
- I enjoy.
- I am nurturing.
- I am happy.

Higher Thought
- I have detoxed the 'diet' word from my mind.
- I expand my mind. I meditate.
- I aspire to issues.
- I learn more.

Filling Up
- I add fruit, vegetables and salad to my diet, so that I feel comfortably full.

Nutrition
- I eat proper meals, packed with vitamins and minerals.

Positive Thinking
- I'm capable without excessive food.
- I'm strong without artificial support.
- I'm able to do anything I want.

Relaxation
- I remember Rome wasn't built in a day.
- I spend time relaxing with my feet up.
- I spend time reading for pleasure.
- I spend time lying in warm bubble baths.

Resolve	■ I approach my weight-loss programme in the same way that I approach my work.
	■ I picture myself in a swimming costume.
Reward	■ I reward myself with happiness and belief in myself.
	■ I reward myself with relaxation.
Rules	■ I eat only as much as I need to satisfy hunger.
	■ It is acceptable to leave food on my plate.
	■ I no longer eat biscuits.
	■ I eat when I am hungry, not for the sake of eating.
Self-respect	■ I recognize and acknowledge my achievements.
Soothing	■ I visualize soft soothing hands stroking my arms and forehead.
Strength	■ I accept love.
	■ I believe in my inner reserves of strength.
	■ It is okay to make mistakes.
	■ I indulge in positive self-talk.
	■ I replace all negative thoughts with positive thoughts.
	■ I take achievements one day at a time.
	■ I let go of worrying about the future, and I stay in the here and now.
Success	■ I congratulate each and every mouthful of success.
	■ I have my confidence back.
	■ I keep the fridge clear of sweet food.
	■ I enjoy the success of wearing clothes with confident ease.
Temptation	■ I tempt you with the fun of life.
	■ I tempt you with good health.
	■ I tempt you with happiness.

Time	■ Remember, darkness and depression are thieves of time.
	■ I take time to consider what to buy and cook.
	■ I take less time eating food for comfort's sake.
	■ I actively get on with tasks that distract me from food.
	■ I take time to look over lists of things and to prioritize what needs to be done.
Treat	■ I love fruit.
	■ I love salads.
	■ I enjoy the effort made to make wonderful food.
Water	■ I drink water to drown the temptation of food.
	■ I drink water as an alternative to wine.
	■ I put the water into the wine glass.
Willpower	■ I set time aside each day to ensure there is something fresh to eat.
	■ I shop properly for wholesome food.
	■ I gradually eat smaller and smaller portions.
	■ I drink glass after glass of cool water to cleanse the system.
	■ I am in the driving seat of my healthy life.
	■ I know when I do not really want something, and I am glad.
Wisdom	■ To eat is to be healthy.
	■ To eat well is to enjoy a sense of wellbeing.
	■ I am increasingly aware.
	■ I focus on the inner substance, the inner nourishment and wellbeing.

The Weighty Blocks

Addiction

Anger

Alcohol

Body image

Cake and custard

Companionship

Craving

Critical

Depression

Devalued

Doubt

Fat

Fear

Greed

Hiding (Hiding doesn't like
change. Anything could happen
if you let go of the weight.
Hiding may agree to come out
providing she gets proper time
to herself.)

Hunger

Inadequate

Insecurity

Lazy

Lack of willpower

Limiting

Lonely

Needy

Pain

Pressure

Punishment

Sadness

Self-saboteur

Stress

Temptation

Tiredness

Uncertainty

Unsatisfied

Weakness

Wrong

Stopping Smoking

This process will involve you in a major detoxification programme. The detox strategy will enable you to work to eliminate those team players who function to derive satisfaction from smoking, and to take control by replacing them with a team of substitutes. Be assured – if you take control and stop smoking you may well wonder what else you can take control of.

You may not be surprised to discover that bad habits are hard to break, given that you may have tried to give up smoking before. To compensate, have you considered what a blessing it is to be able to keep good ones?

Imagine learning to drive a car, and then suddenly losing the habit! Or learning to walk as a child and then suddenly forgetting!

To form a habit, you practise it and, when practised enough, it becomes automatic. You first consciously work at it, then, if you continue for a sufficient length of time, the inner mind takes over and you perform the habit unconsciously. As a child you consciously learned to tie shoelaces. Now it is an unconscious action, one performed in seconds. Whether the habit is good or bad for you is of no particular concern to the inner mind, until *you* decide otherwise. When *you* do decide you want to put an end to a habit, you have to practise again until you stop doing it.

Smoking is very much a habit. Most people smoke at certain times of the day and their habit has become routine in certain situations. Many situations create an association with smoking. Of paramount importance in kicking the smoking habit is to break these associations – a cigarette with a drink, a cigarette after a meal, a cigarette as a reward, a way of marking time for yourself.

Amongst the rank and file of your inner team are members that run your bad habit. Like a racket, they have an interest in it. There they lurk in the no-changing room, locked away so as to frustrate the pathway to Quitting. They are like a hit squad, dead set on course to kill you. You may once again ask yourself, as captain, why you tolerate them at all. And of course they will chorus: Addiction, Habit, Nicotine, Death Wish. Remember, you are in charge, *so why do you tolerate them at all?* Pleasure and Enjoyment pipe in. Are you prepared to play to their tune too?

Okay, so perhaps you've tried to stop before. Perhaps you've lined them all up and marched them into the No Smoking room. Did they wonder what was going on? Long ago, when you first started smoking, it wasn't a bad habit, because you wanted to do it. Now, suddenly, you're telling them it's a bad habit and you want to give up. 'Can't you make up your mind?' they say.

Resistance rounds them up. The outcome – some, perhaps all, refuse to give up. 'It's New Year. It's the right thing to do. You know that. Bring in the cheer and stop smoking. C'mon guys. Give me a break. It's my health see …' 'We'll try,' they lie. By two in the morning they are protesting. They are urging you on – stirring you up like crazy. Resistance has arranged a protest. You stand up and give them a dressing down. 'Listen guys, after all it's only two hours into the match.' You arrange to transfer in a great team from the back rooms, a team which in the past has promised you success. Sure they need a bit of a shake up and a dust down, and a talking to – and they listen. They agree to play by the rules. New Year Resolution, Money-up-in-Smoke, Health, Holiday, New Car, Clothes, Social. They play full-out. Seeking redress, the smokers drive you up the wall with Frustration and Tension. You feel run out and stressed out. Comfort eats you out of house and home. No way is Fat coming back. You concede you've lost the match and light up a cigarette.

The inner smoking team, whilst *you* were happy to continue smoking, were in harmony. Though you do not wish to smoke, the inner team of smokers continue to get satisfaction from smoking. When you took the cigarettes away, it was like taking a dangerous toy away from a small child. The team rebelled as a child may scream. The team continued to push to smoke, as a child may search for another toy to play with. The child is not looking around for a bad toy or a good one, just a toy, but it may choose a toy that is even more dangerous. Similarly you, the smoker, simmer with Frustration and Stress. You then summon Comfort, get Fat and lose in the face of so much Resistance.

When the child screams you would naturally give the child another toy. If this new toy is as entertaining as the old one, the child will once again become absorbed in play. When you removed the cigarettes, if you had a substitute team in place who were playing full-out for the benefits and advantages of the new habit, and relishing every moment of it, Resistance would be more likely to stay away. With Resistance less likely to kick in you are much better placed to create and embed the new habit.

In rapport with your inner mind, you can recruit a team of substitutes to support your decision to stop. Once the satisfaction has been taken away from the inner smoking team and transferred over to your inner team of substitutes, the cigarettes will increasingly be anything but enjoyable.

First off, you need to identify a great team of substitutes. Let's look over some proven successful substitutes, and the suggestions each came up with.

Benefits	■	I feel healthy and healthier.
	■	I have fewer coughs and colds.
	■	I enjoy fresh-smelling clothes.
	■	Overflowing ashtrays are dirty and ugly.
	■	I am free of addiction.
Comfort	■	I have more self-esteem.
	■	I can afford more material comforts.
	■	I am free of drugs.
Control	■	I am in control of something that controlled me.
	■	I am in control of my life.
	■	My life will be as I want.
	■	It is my body.
Conform	■	I support your decision.
	■	I remember the positive aspects.
	■	I let go, and sense your freedom – a form of rebellion.
Cool	■	I enjoy food.
	■	I enjoy sex.
	■	I enjoy sport.
	■	I enjoy being outdoors.
Creative	■	I no longer hide behind cigarettes.

Determination
- I have the stamina to stop smoking.
- I have the desire to stop smoking.
- I have the confidence to stop smoking.
- I have the inner greatness to stop smoking.

Diet
- I eat cleaner and fresher food.
- I have more energy to create more appetizing meals.

Energy
- The more energy I have, the better my body feels.
- The better my body feels, the more energy I have.

Enjoyment
- I read in the evening.
- I walk more during the day.
- I listen to music whilst travelling in the car.
- I always listen to music in bad traffic.
- I enjoy the money I save.
- I appreciate all the natural benefits of the Earth.

Friendship
- I keep busy.
- I spend more time outside.
- I decide to study or take a course.

Family
- Myself and my family are free of my smoke.

Focus
- I focus on the feeling of wellbeing.
- I focus on the benefits of being a non-smoker.

Hands
- I have more time to take good care of my hands.
- I exercise my hands.
- I have more time to write.

Happy
- I have more energy.
- I have more opportunities to enjoy.
- I am fitter.
- I am able to smile.

Health	■ My organs will live for longer now they are free.
	■ I am free from fear of ill-health.
	■ I feel less damaged inside.
	■ I breathe more easily.
	■ My throat is relieved of pain.
	■ I no longer wheeze.
	■ I feel cleaner.
	■ I feel fresher.
	■ I no longer have to stand out in the cold.
	■ I sense the air, the mountains, the grass.
	■ I enjoy being more intimate.
Higher Thought	■ I am cleaner.
	■ I am free of smell.
Laughter	■ I can smile whenever I feel like it.
	■ I am free to laugh whenever I want to.
	■ I let go.
	■ I'm seen more.
	■ I'm being present more.
Life	■ I participate in more outdoor activity.
	■ I take more exercise.
	■ I cut down on stimulants and sugar.
	■ I take the time to do more things I enjoy.
Money	■ My savings are growing.
	■ Motivated.
	■ I am free of the coughing fits.
	■ I take responsibility to stop damaging my family.
	■ I am able to exercise to become fitter.
	■ I repeat, 'I'm no longer a smoker'.

No	■	Everything is cleaner.
	■	I'm proud.
Occupied	■	I am fully occupied at work.
	■	I talk about having stopped with non-smokers.
Organized	■	I set goals to do it.
	■	I am taking action now.
Positive	■	I do it.
Purity	■	I am freer and cleaner.
	■	I am free of the crutch.
	■	I am clear.
Reassurance	■	My emotions remain calm, now I am free of the prop.
	■	I feel fine without the prop.
Relaxation	■	I relax in healthy ways.
Strength	■	I've decided to live.
	■	I enjoy life free of cigarettes.
	■	I breathe more easily.
	■	I communicate with love.
	■	I feel happier.
Social	■	I consider the meal enhanced without a cigarette.
Success	■	I'm proud of myself.
	■	I'm going on holiday.
	■	I have more energy.
	■	I am more positive.
	■	I am more healthy.

Taste Buds	■ Cigarettes taste horrible.
	■ I taste the good in life and in everything.
	■ My mouth tastes better.
Time	■ I have more time.
	■ I have time to be more involved in physical activity.
	■ I spend time with people who do not smoke.
	■ Time is too valuable to smoke it away.
	■ If I can do it for a week, then I can do it for a month.
Trust	■ I trust in myself to succeed.
	■ I trust I can do it.
Willpower	■ I remember why I'm stopping (health, pregnancy).
	■ I remember the bad effects.
	■ I remember the expense.
	■ I remember the dirty ashtrays.
	■ I remember feeling sick.
	■ I remember to keep my hands busy.
	■ I ensure you experience fully the benefits of not smoking.
Wise	■ I have a wonderful vision of life.

Now let us expose some of the team members who keep you inhaling the poisons and toxins, and undermine your will to quit.

Examine the list below. Some of these players are positive team members involved in a deadly pursuit. They are players who have lived and experienced themselves via a habit that will eventually kill you. They are, however, essentially positive at the best of times and well worth having around. These team members will be encouraged to come forward with suggestions to create their same feeling and outcome by thinking or behaving in another way. One that is healthy and of positive benefit to you. As you look through the list, you will notice Company in the line up. A generation ago, one advertising slogan ran, 'You're never alone with a Strand'. Decades on, companionship is one reason given by some people for why they smoke.

 A team member who encouraged Julie to smoke did so as a Friend in Friendship. With some coaching she came forward with other ways of offering friendship ...

'I listen in quiet times.'

'I compliment you on your achievements.'

'I nourish you now, whereas I used to destroy you.'

'I am there. Quietly. I communicate with love.'

Happy is noted in the line-up too. Again, this may not appear so surprising. Another advertisement has sold us the line for years that 'Happiness is a cigar called Hamlet'. Some smokers have attributed a happy feeling, and situations, to cigarettes. Indeed, advertising continues to spin us these roguish persuasions, and we continue to buy them.

The 'butt' can stop here! The 'butt' can stop with you!

When you've resolved to stop smoking, it will be necessary to encourage and to coach that portion of Happy that attributes being happy with smoking to be happy in other ways. These other ways may be other ways of behaving, thinking or doing – ways that are life-enabling and life-ennobling – ways that do not involve smoking cigarettes, or cigars, or indeed any other nicotine substitutes. Be assured that *your* sense of Happy will come forward with other ways of sensing happiness in you, and in your life, some of which may be included in the earlier list, and others which may be quite different. Tailor-made. Custom made. Couture.

Here are the team members that work against you giving up:

Accessory

Addiction

Alcohol

Boredom

Calm

Childish

Comfort

Company

Confident

Craving

Defiance

Drinking

Emptiness

Friendship

Frustration

Habit

Happy

Hunger

Irritation

Lonely

Nicotine

Pathetic

Pressure

Protection (the belief that smoke creates a smoke screen between yourself and others, that smoke keeps people at a distance).

Rebellion (to retain some sense of self by following one's own spirit, and not doing what is demanded by authority).

Restlessness

Routine

Secret smoker

Self-esteem

Social

Solitary/Alone

Stress

Telephone sales/Talk

Tension

Tobacco

Urge

Weight

Withdrawal

Rogue players will be eliminated outright in the course of the detox process. You may find that the process works initially in allowing you to cut down, that your interest dwindles as the positive, healthful players take up position. Each day's detox will add one or two more supportive team members. It follows that as more players join your champion team with the expressed intention to stop smoking, the evidence of your success will grow. You will begin to notice a difference and eventually you will be in control of a team playing full out to keep you free.

From time to time, an away game in a bar, a restaurant and the like, may exert pressure. What if you give in? I suggest to you that one cigarette, now you are a non-smoker, does not a smoker make you. Coach your thoughts in a way that transcends the insidious voice that says, 'Well I've had one so I've failed ... I may as well have another ...' Coach your inner team along different lines. One of your saboteurs just stepped back onto your previously 'level' playing field – more than likely a potentially positive player – Social for example. Excited and buoyant. So now you are a non-smoker with a player whose temporary lapse has disturbed balanced and healthy play.

Keeping these thoughts in mind, find a moment just to check in (if you can) to the detox coaching room – maybe on a trip to the loo.

Close your eyes. From within, suggest which player has disturbed play. Do some coaching there and then. It is prime time to get your inner team back on track, and follow-up with further coaching next day and the next. Remember you are a great team.

Anxiety and Stress

Many of us feel a sense of anxiety, which may be directed towards something in particular that we see as threatening, or it may be vague and unattached but no less intense for that. We may feel we have the potential to progress, but there seems to be a barrier that prevents us from moving forward, or an invisible shackle of anxiety that holds us back. Spontaneous fun with family and friends can be restricted by thoughts and feelings focused on what others think. Anxiety is very often accompanied by feelings of insecurity, a sense of feeling afraid of small things. Experiences of anxiety and stress can range from feeling unpleasant sensations in the body to physiological complaints like repetitive strain injury (RSI), irritable bowel syndrome (IBS), an aching jaw, and pain in the shoulders, neck and back. You may have a tendency to clutch and grasp onto objects too tightly, such as the steering wheel when driving

your car, or to grind your teeth. Some discover that they have unconsciously been 'holding their breath', waiting for news of something bad
happening or about to happen to them. Unresolved 'obsessive thinking'
and 'inner turmoil' can create a lack of focus, an inability to concentrate,
and insomnia.

As a first giant step towards combating all of these symptoms, follow
through with one of two options. Create an Orange Liquid Detox tape
using the script in Chapter 6. Alternatively, listen to the prepared
companion tape to *Mind Detox* a couple of times each and every week. It
will work wonders for you! I would go so far as to describe it as a 'verbal'
massage – massaging you from the top of your head to the tip of your
toes. Take the time to do this and you will naturally begin the process of
rinsing down your relationship with yourself.

Anxiety and stress are activated by a sense of striving to feel safe, to
feel protected from danger, to be in control of unresolved events and
experiences in your life. And it can be attached to a life sentence as
discussed in Chapter 11.

These conditions can bring forward players that appear alarming and
stir anxiety but nonetheless somehow exist to create states that are life-
enabling and fulfilling. A player named Danger may be making a person
anxious, having been seeded in the inner mind during childhood in situations when playful exploration on climbing frames and low-lying walls
was oft described as dangerous. A child who heard the sentence 'You will
fall down and hurt yourself' may well be more disposed to a sense of
prevailing danger.

It is fair to say, though, that an appropriate awareness of danger and of
the potential for danger is essential in the inner mind. The conversation
with this particular team player may involve firstly suggesting that it is
the cause of an undercurrent of anxiousness that is failing to serve you in
the present. You may continue to say that now you have resolved to move
forward in your life and free yourself of anxiety, you require this player to
support the change, and not to hinder it. The player is very likely to agree

to support you. You may be surprised at the suggestions that come forward, which can channel the same energy into a beneficial use. For example, Danger comes forward with suggestions – to protect, to be watchful, to serve you and to be bold. Listen!

Bubble-bursting and Stress-busting

Throughout the day, you may periodically choose to go within. Once within, gather all of the negative stress and tension of the past few hours into a bubble. Next, visualize popping the bubble with a needle. Sense the bubble bursting, and the mental toxins dispersing far, far away. Perhaps they metamorphose into flower petals, snowflakes, feathers – something symbolic of lightness and the beauty of life. What is important is that you puncture the barrier and release the pressure on yourself, and let go of a force that sometimes feels like it is about to burst in you or upon someone else. Burst it safely in a way that protects you and your health, and the close family member or colleague who may be in line to feel the force of your pressure. Burst a few bubbles. Then begin the difficult discussion. That way it is less likely to go awry because of your emotional upheaval.

Whichever way you choose to cleanse and rinse anxiety away, the most important thing is that you do it. Our bodies have to cope with the pollution in our external world. They can adapt and cope with this, and can cope better with help and support from the fresh and clean food we choose to eat. Additionally, you can help by freeing your body of those thoughts that pollute your sense of calm, and your sense of being present. This is your diet for your mind. As you are what you eat, you are the thoughts you digest.

The Clement Team

Calm
- I breathe slowly.
- I relax my muscles.
- I sense the bigger picture.

Confidence
- I let go of worry when I make mistakes.
- I follow what I sense is right for me.
- I dwell on positive things.

Joyful
- I look forward to being in the present.
- I concentrate on those things that are worth doing.
- I forgive people who have done wrong.
- I face new challenges free of fear.
- I allow for and learn from mistakes.
- I remind you to be happy.

Protection
- I give myself permission to relax.
- I share responsibilities with others.
- I rinse away personal criticism.

Relaxation
- Music calms and relaxes me.
- I breathe more slowly.
- I sit down and meditate.

The Inclement Team
- Anger.
- Anxiety.
- Control.
- Danger.
- Frustration.
- Perfection.
- Restriction.
- Ridicule.
- Stress.
- Tense.

Public Speaking and Presentations

'The idea of making a presentation makes me feel …' Complete that sentence in no more than two words!

For those of you who welcomed words like 'excited', 'wonderful', 'passionate', 'pleased', you may read what follows with interest, for you may once have trodden in these same steps. To those of you who thought of anything other than fabulous words when filling in the sentence above, read on and take action.

Did the words that came to your mind speak of a dry mouth, a beating heart, racked nerves, anxiousness, fear? Public speaking is an experience that for many elicits anxiety, fear and panic. A person is more than likely to include one of these three words in their personal story of how public speaking affects them – both when they actually do it, and when they imagine doing it.

Seminars, talks, presentations, training sessions, product information roadshows, meetings, and speeches to celebrate the contributions of departing colleagues, or family occasions like weddings, christenings and special birthdays: all may require words to be spoken in front of more than one, two or three people.

Can you imagine speaking with calm and passion – with an easy sense of joy and enjoyment? In today's world, public speaking is regarded as a key skill, one that some companies develop in their employees, and one that other companies ask potential employees to possess already. Today it is not uncommon for a job applicant to be asked to give a formal presentation in front of an interview panel as part of the selection process.

 Jeremy worked as a business financier and, following a company merger, he was looking for a new job. During his search for suitable roles he found that the majority required an increased public-speaking role. Jeremy was no newcomer to public speaking. His previous position had demanded that he undertake speaking engagements on an occasional basis. He reported that the days, even weeks, before the event could be a tormenting period. During the application process he found it 'impossible to shut down the Worry'. He could find 'no lasting comfort', and eventually the Worry began to impact on his Self-confidence and his sense of Courage. On the positive side, he shared that he was always very well prepared for public-speaking events and that 'Once I get into [the speech], I do a good job'. Despite these past successes, however, the negative messages proved overwhelming, and he found it impossible to counteract them. Definitely there was a gremlin somewhere in Jeremy's mental mechanics. And indeed there was! The spanner in the works was the opinion and view of a healthy, self-aware, independent and opinionated nine-year-old who had been forced, much against his better judgement, to dress up as a garden gnome for an infant school play. 'How stupid can you be?', he exclaimed, 'a garden gnome!', and in his defence, 'I tried to get out of it', and finally resolved, 'Once was enough!'

This mere sprite of a young lad was able to summon the sense of looking Stupid, a sense of humiliation and of Torment, Worry and Fear, which collectively virtually struck down Courage and Confidence. The memory was in many ways like a life sentence. 'Once [on the stage, in the presence of many watching] was enough!', an overwhelmingly powerful message to the inner mind that was working overtime in the present. Moreover, although Jeremy protested that he had 'tried to get out of it', there was a sense of his being judged as not having tried hard enough – a sense that Jeremy still harboured a grudge against the youngster. Jeremy needed help polishing the jewels! Indeed, he needed to work to bring himself up-to-date. The truth was he had long outgrown the garden gnome costume he was still wearing! He had, however, not outgrown his sense of outrage with his younger self for not getting out of the play. How could his younger self let him look so stupid? A Wise Being, together with a sense of Forgiveness, Acceptance and Understanding of his younger self by his older self, were necessary to free him from an automatic association of public speaking with the young green gnome. Now in the present, he was able to begin to coach those players afresh.

Yes, there are public speaking engagements that the majority would stretch themselves to accomplish – events when you are chosen to be best man or woman at a friend's wedding, say. With such engagements, it seems that the burden of letting the side down is heavier than doing your duty.

For most of us the mere thought of standing in front of people and speaking can generate feelings and sensations of panic and dizziness. Sarah shared her experience of a presentation: ' I couldn't eat lunch. My entire feeling was focused on the build-up and generally knowing I was next.' We worry about forgetting everything we prepared, and if we make it to the end, worry about not being able to answer the questions from the audience. The ability to relax seems to vanish. A person can be so focused on the spoken word, that thoughts and feelings get locked up. Confusion creates a fog of incoherence. To avoid panic-fired incoherence, you may decide to read the words and doggedly focus on a prepared script.

Others seek to avoid it! 'Not me! No way am I doing that!' Fear takes over and all your other supportive players go Absent Without Leave. They run for cover to the no-changing room. Fear organizes a rally. Humiliation, Failure, Pain, Rejection, Abandonment, and others attend and it feels like you are under threat as all of your greatest fears collude. Then, just when you thought there was no way out, Creative comes up with an excuse to get you off the hook. Reassurance speaks up for you: 'They'll find someone else to do it.' You acknowledge some Guilt, and a sense of lost Opportunity. There the two of them lurk to remind you of your loss. In turn you remind yourself that those two players feel less painful than public speaking. These thoughts are short-lived. Often what lurks on a deeper level is the thought that in some sense you have let yourself down. There is an underlying suspicion that as you were asked to give the talk in the first place, the person who asked you must have thought you were capable of preparing and delivering the talk. This is the Truth. This is the truth of your greater Clarity and your Heart's Understanding. You might just have done it! You may just have been great!

You slowly come to realize that by not changing your mind, and by not risking yourself, and by not seizing the opportunity and giving yourself the choice of change, you ultimately experience more pain than in the risking. You lose 'yourself' without having played the game.

> Our deepest fear is not that we are inadequate, our deepest fear is that we are powerful beyond measure. It is our light not our darkness that most frightens us. We ask ourselves, who am I to be brilliant, gorgeous and talented? Actually, who are you not to be? It is not just in some of us –it is in everyone. And, as we let our own light shine, we unconsciously give permission for other people to do the same. As we are liberated from our fear our presence automatically liberates others. You are a child of God. Playing small doesn't serve the world. There is nothing enlightening about shrinking, so that other people won't feel insecure around you. We are meant to shine in life, like children do. We were born to manifest the glory of God within us.
>
> Nelson Mandela

Doing a few Mind Detox sessions to coach a team of key players may give you the back-up and support you need to go out there and give it your best – to go forward with a team that could kick Fear into touch.

The players profiled below are those who came forward and said 'Yes' to public speaking. These players stepped forward to support team captains who, in the words of Dr Susan Jeffers, decided to 'Feel the Fear and Do it Anyway'.

Take on board those team members, and the suggestions they make, combined with the suggestions that come forward from your team – and look forward to the next opportunity to speak in public!

The Performance Team

Anticipation   ■   I enjoy the sense of anticipation.

Assured   ■   I look smart.

           ■   I have a clear voice.

Belief	■ I believe everyone wants me to succeed.
Build-up	■ I maintain relaxation.
Calm	■ My hands are steady.
	■ My arms are by my side.
	■ I am projecting my voice.
	■ I am standing straight and relaxed.
	■ My posture is good.
Communication	■ I step back mentally. I think and then answer.
	■ I remind you there is no rush. There is no hurry.
Confidence	■ I believe in you …
	■ I am at one with the audience.
	■ My audience have confidence in what I have to say.
	■ When I do not know the answer to a question I will be honest and say so. I'll say I'll come back with an answer having found out, and I do.
	■ I am comfortable, calm and confident.
Energy	■ I sense the energy from the audience.
	■ I sense the support of my work colleagues.
	■ I take exercise and stretch before I speak.
	■ I drink plenty of water.
Focus	■ I concentrate on the positive.
Heavy and Big	■ I encourage you to imagine wearing big, wooden, comfortable and solid shoes to ground you.
Heartbeat	■ I maintain your heartbeat at a normal level.
	■ I listen.
	■ I remain calm.

Belief	■ I believe everyone wants me to succeed.
Preparation	■ I will enjoy a relaxing evening before the presentation.
	■ I will enjoy nice food before the presentation.
	■ I will have a good night's sleep
	■ I'm excited and looking forward to tomorrow.
Professional	■ I'll prepare.
	■ I'll enjoy the experience.
	■ I sit straight.
	■ I smile.
	■ I am calm.
	■ I am assured.
	■ I enjoy the performance.
Remembering	■ I write key words and phrases on postcard-sized cards.
	■ I use an overhead projector to aid memory.
	■ The audience will be in rapport and responding.
	■ Audience questions will remind me that I know a lot.
Speech	■ I speak well.
	■ I speak with confidence.
	■ I believe my speech is interesting.
	■ I remind you to think before you speak.
	■ I structure your thoughts so you can communicate.
	■ The speech runs as smoothly as a conversation.
	■ I help you breathe more slowly.
	■ I help you relax.

Strength	■ I focus on your strengths.
	■ I help you face rather than hide from mistakes.
	■ I am a blanket around you.
	■ I am the feeling of a group.
	■ I am singing and playing your tune.
	■ When I sit straight I feel strong.
Support	■ I'll be there alongside you.
	■ I suggest to you that you have strong support (this strength may come from one or more friends or relatives, one or an army of imaginary wise beings standing at your side and around you. They form a chain of energy and strength, holding you in your power whilst you speak).
	■ I am a companion – a hand to hold on to.
Wisdom	■ I move your focus from yourself to your audience.

The Presenting Problem Team

Dizzy
Fear
Forgetful
Isolation
Knees
Nervous
Perfectionism
Stomach
Stress
Worry

Team Spirit

While we are thinking about team spirit, I would like to make reference to a novel, *The Fifth Mountain*, by Paulo Coelho. I was curious to absorb the concluding stages of his story, and I sense that mention of them here is appropriate. The hero, Elijah, is coaching a reluctant team of players to rebuild a city and a future. The team is assembled slowly, and each member is persuaded to cast off Futility, Daunted, Scepticism, Past and Abject Future. A woman, an old man, a boy, a woman, more old men and women gather to re-member how to re-create, to re-claim and re-gain team spirit.

Inspired by the wisdom of a shepherd, Elijah coaches the team to let go of the practice of moving into the future whilst remaining engrossed in the past. He encourages them towards freedom – to build a beautiful future. As the building project gathers momentum, the prophet invites each of the assembled team to choose 'a new name, beginning at this very moment'. He continues by saying, 'This will be the sacred name that brings together in a single word all that [the people] have dreamed of fighting for.' He shares that, 'For my name I have chosen *Liberation*.'

The people in the square were silent for some time. Then the woman who had been the first to help Elijah rose to her feet.

'My name is Re-encounter,' she said.

'My name is Wisdom,' said an old man.

The son of the widow whom Elijah had loved shouted, 'My name is Alphabet.'

Regular Mind Detoxing will wake you up. It will help bring you back to life – bring you back to a state of being more conscious to choose, and choose more wisely. The more aware you are of the words, the life sentences and the circulating thoughts inside, the more you can choose consciously to coach them to create a more positive and more honest state of mind, or let them go. Initially you will have consciously to set aside time to detox – time and again to coach, to revise and edit some of the driving forces in your inner mind. The more you do this the more you will become aware of the choices you are making all the time with the thoughts that pass too quickly or quietly for you to catch or scrutinize. When redesigned, these conscious choices will bring you ever closer to acknowledging the truth of your captaining a team with a higher purpose and hence a team playing in a different and higher league. You will gain in cupfuls the benefits and advantages of moving into that higher league, and higher consciousness.

With this consciousness of choice-making (as opposed to unconsciousness of it), will come an increasing awareness and acknowledgement of the illusions that have been coached within us by the captains of the external world. No longer will you be a victim of your choices. Increasingly you will be a stronger and more confident champion of them. Your true sense of self-expression will speak from within, rather than from without. It will lead you away from the idea of self-expression and emotional mood-swings as by-products or adjuncts to changing the colour of the outer casing of our mobile phones; the colour and patterning of our contact lenses, watch straps, or the flashings on our trainers. These will hold less marketable weight.

This empowering experience will heighten our intuitive awareness of the choices we make, their impact, and our responsibility for them and for the life we create. As you open to lightening your mental load, your physical and material load may lighten too. Your need and reliance on external vehicles to create the fully expressed you will loosen their grip and adhesion as you begin to listen to, and hear the coaching of the captain within. Your whole inner mind will flow with team spirit.

Choose a name to represent you and your inner team – one you will overlay on their team colours as each team member plays full-out for you and your life!

Afterword

The notion of Mind Detox, and particularly of building an inner team, is a metaphor, a metaphor that restructures the landscape of your inner mind. It is a metaphor to encourage a process utilizing clean language – words, phrases and vocabulary familiar to you, together with symbolic shapes to provide entry into a symbolic world that lies just outside awareness.

In adopting the inner-team metaphor, your aims have been to detox stuck and toxic states and promote personal changes, be these of behaviour, ideas, thoughts, habits or feelings in a variety of situations and circumstances. Curious and enlightening information has become available to you, helping you to be increasingly conscious to make new choices and change behaviours.

The notion of building an inner team was inspired by a process known as 'Parts Therapy', the term 'parts' alluding to 'parts of the mind', another therapeutic metaphor. Parts Therapy has been employed by past masters of therapeutic hypnosis, over the last three decades, by Virginia Satir and Charles Tebbetts to name but two. Both practised a form of symbolic interactive hypnotherapy, as do many other practitioners today. In recent years, Parts Therapy has been incorporated into the techniques of Neuro-Linguistic Programming (NLP), which has been co-developed by Richard Bandler and John Grinder.

The ideas included presuppose that the inner mind has an enabling function as opposed to a prohibitive one. Your inner mind becomes apparent when in deep relaxation. It is the part of the mind that enables you to do so many of the things that you would find impossible to do consciously – sustaining the beat of your heart, the breath in your lungs, walking and running smoothly, or catching a ball, finding your way through familiar streets, recognizing old friends, and tying up your shoelaces. It is the place wherein resides your individual body wisdom, and your body clock.

Mind Detox has offered an interpretative, symbolic process of coaching to promote an inner dialogue that encourages personal change, clarity, understanding, acceptance and personal peace. Rather than a peace that 'passeth all understanding', it is a peace that is borne of clarity and understanding.

The vocabulary may not be scientific, although the words are interpretively plausible. The technique may be judged on its subtlety, its plausibility and its efficacy. Because you are dealing with feelings as a feeling being, a different sort of conversation is in order. The words are interpreted in a way that is most meaningful for you, so they are sensed as beng perfectly plausible and sensible.

Mind Detox is an interpretative process designed to move you, to illuminate you, and to increase your sense and understanding of what it is like to be a truly fearless and freely expressive you, each and every day of your life. As the adage goes, 'Today is the first day of the rest of your life'.

Bibliography

Andreas, Steve and Faulkner, Charles. *Technology of Achievement*, London, Nicholas Brealey Publishing, 1996

Austin, Valerie. *Self Hypnosis*, London, Thorsons, 1994

Austin, Valerie. *Free Yourself from Fear*, London, Thorsons, 1998

Brahma Kumaris. *Virtue Reality* cards

Bunyan, John. *The Pilgrim's Progress*, London, Penguin Books, 1987

Coelho, Paulo. *The Alchemist*, London, HarperCollins, 1996

Coelho, Paulo. *The Fifth Mountain*, London, HarperCollins, 1998

Connolly, David. *In Search of Angels*, New York, Perigee Books, 1993

Eckersley, Glennyce S. *An Angel at My Shoulder: True Stories of Angelic Experiences*, London, Rider, 1996

Hastings, Julia. *You Can Have What You Want*, London, Touchstone Publications Ltd, 1992

Hay, Louise. *The Power is Within You*, Enfield, Eden Grove Editions, 1991

Janki, Dadi. *Wings of Soul: Emerging Your Spiritual Identity*, London, Brahma Kumaris Information Services, 1998

Jeffers, Susan. *End the Struggle and Dance with Life*, London, Hodder & Stoughton, 1996

Jeffers, Susan. *Feel the Fear and Do It Anyway*, London, Rider, 1997

The Jerusalem Bible, Popular Edition, Darton, Longman and Todd, 1995

Milne, A.A. *Winnie the Pooh*, London, Methuen & Co. Ltd, 1926

Norwood, Robin. *Why Me? Why This? Why Now?*, London, Random House, 1995

Peck, M. Scott. *The Road Less Travelled and Beyond*, New York, Simon & Schuster, 1997

Roget, Peter M. *Thesaurus of English Words and Phrases*, Penguin, 1998 (originally published 1852)

Soskin, Julie. *Alignment to Light*, Bath, Ashgrove Press, 1994

Trungpa, Chögyam. *First Thought, Best Thought*, Boston, Shambhala Press, 1984

Walsch, Neale Donald. *Meditations from 'Conversations with God' book 1*, London, Hodder & Stoughton, 1997

Weil, Andrew. *Spontaneous Healing*, London, Warner Books, 1995

Films

Fleming, Victor (director). *The Wizard of Oz*, Metro-Goldwyn-Mayer, 1939, based on the book by L. Frank Baum

Stevenson, Robert (director). *Mary Poppins*, Walt Disney, 1964; based on the book *Mary Poppins* by P.L. Travers, 1934

Wenders, Wim (director). *Wings of Desire (Der Himmel über Berlin)*, Argos Films and the British Film Institute, 1987 (A Hollywood remake, *City of Angels*, was released by Warner Brothers in 1998.)

Useful Addresses

UK

Whole-Being Hypnotherapy
155 Sumatra Road
London
NW6 1PN
web address http://www.ursasoft.com/hypno/
Tel: 0171 432 0307

Whole-Being Hypnotherapy clinics are also available at:

The Harbour Club Total Health Clinic
Watermeadow Lane
London
SW6 2RR
Tel: 0171 371 7744

The Laboratory Spa and Health Clubs
The Avenue
London
N10 2QJ
Tel: 0181 482 4000

For a list of approved practising hypnotherapists in your area write enclosing a stamped addressed envelope to:
The Registrar
The Hypnotherapy Research Society
Millfield Business Centre
Stone in Oxney
Kent
TN30 7JL
Tel: 01580 765856

Brahma Kumaris World Spiritual University
Global Co-operation House
65 Pound Lane
London
NW10 2HH
Tel: 0181 459 1400

The Brahma Kumaris offer Meditation, Stress Management and Positive Thinking courses throughout the UK. Books, tapes and CDs are available from BK Publications at the address above.

The Austin Training Centres
10 Harley Street
London
W1N 1AA
0181 569 7192

USA

American Council of Hypnotherapist Examiners
1147 East Broadway
Suite 340, Glendale
CA 91205

Canada

The Canadian Institute of Ethical Hypnosis
Suite 104
Camelot
1817–14A Street SW
Calgary
Alberta
T2T 3W7

Australia

The Australian Society of Hypnosis
Austin Medical Centre*
Heidelberg
Victoria, 3084

* Please note that the above organisation is not connected in any way with the Austin
Training Centres.

Index